Collins *practical gardener*

3

practical gardener

WATER
GARDENING

GRAHAM CLARKE

First published in 2004 by HarperCollins*Publishers*

77–85 Fulham Palace Road, London, W6 8JB

The Collins website address is:

www.collins.co.uk

Text by Graham Clarke; copyright © HarperCollins*Publishers*

Artworks and design © HarperCollins*Publishers*

Photography by Tim Sandall and Graham Clarke

Cover photography by Tim Sandall

Photographic props: Coolings Nurseries, Rushmore Hill,
Knockholt, Kent, TN14 7NN, www.coolings.co.uk

Thanks also to Polhill Garden Centre, Badgers Mount,
Sevenoaks, Kent TN14 7BD for additional assistance

Design and editorial: Focus Publishing, Sevenoaks, Kent

Project editor: Guy Croton

Editor: Vanessa Townsend

Project co-ordinator: Caroline Watson

Design & illustration: David Etherington

For HarperCollins

Senior managing editor: Angela Newton

Design manager: Luke Griffin

Editor: Alastair Laing

Editorial assistant: Lisa John

Production: Chris Gurney

A CIP catalogue record for this book is available from the
British Library

ISBN 000716405X

Colour reproduction by Colourscan

Printed and bound in Italy by L.E.G.O.

Contents

Introduction

Mankind has always used water – in the main, of course, to stay alive. In the hustle and bustle of 21st century living, however, we generally consider bodies of water to be good for our souls: havens of tranquillity and serenity in a technologically manic world. Hundreds of thousands of people take their annual vacations to visit great lakes, meandering rivers and even mountain streams – to recharge their batteries and take in the clean air: to attempt to become one with Nature.

The early gardeners recognized the potential of water as both a symbolic and decorative element, and it rapidly became a feature of their gardens.

A sculpture, found by historians in Mesopotamia, and thought to be around 4,000 years old, appears to have been used as a fountain. If so, it was the prototype of the ornamental fountains seen today in our parks and gardens.

Around 3,000 years ago in China, during the Shang dynasty, many gardens were created that incorporated water. The Yin-Yang symbol – the two opposing forces of life – were represented by water and rock. And 2,500 years ago, Islamic garden 'designers' used two intersecting canals to create a geometric garden; it represented the four rivers of paradise and the elements of water, fire, air and earth.

Today, the appeal of a garden pond (or some such water feature), comes down to two essential things.

There are few more pleasing and serene garden features than a pond

First, it serves up an undisputed combination of beauty and serenity which, actually, are hard to distinguish between.

Second, all water gardeners, no matter how 'devout' are fascinated to discover, and to encourage, the secret hidden world that is teeming with life and interest down amongst the depths. Yes, water gardening is as much about enjoying another 'world', as it is about looking after goldfish, installing filters and planting water irises.

Most of the plants featured in this book are grown for their beautiful displays of flowers and/or foliage. Whereas some need to have their roots permanently under water, others like to be planted in the garden soil. All of them, however, need the wet or damp conditions afforded by a pond or its edges.

It is our aim in this book to show that there are many facets to a garden water feature. We cover rules to adhere to, and offer ideas to copy – and most are well within the capabilities of gardeners.

Water can be combined with floral colour to create stunning effects

How to Use This Book

This book is divided into several sections. The opening chapter guides you through all the practical considerations of gardening with aquatic plants, including choosing and buying plants, how to construct and maintain a pond, general plant care and propagation techniques. A comprehensive plant directory follows, divided into the several categories of aquatic plants, covering oxygenating, floating, flowering,

marginal and bog plants as well as ferns and grasses. Nearly 200 plants are covered, and all are arranged in alphabetical order within their respective categories. The final section of the book covers planting combinations, fish, koi and wildlife. Troubleshooting pages allow you to diagnose the likely cause of any problems, and a directory of pests and diseases offers advice on how to solve them.

latin name of the plant genus, followed by its **common name**

detailed descriptions give specific advice on care for each plant, including pruning and pests and diseases

alphabetical tabs on the side of the page, colour-coded to help you quickly find the plant you want

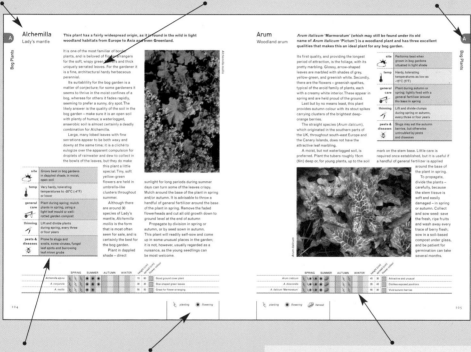

care charts provide an at-a-glance summary of the plant's specific needs (N.B. Where more than one genus appear on the page, the chart may cater for both plants)

a key at the bottom of the page explains what each symbol means

variety charts list recommended varieties for most genera of water garden plants that feature more than one variety. These display key information to help you choose your ideal plant, showing:

• when (or if) the plant is in flower during the year
• the time to plant for the best results
• when interesting nuts, berries or other fruit appear
• the height and spread after optimum growth
• the principle colour of the flowers (or foliage)
• additional comments from the author

Assessing Your Garden

Existing features

Your garden is unique in the opportunities that it has to offer and the constraints that it might impose. So before you install your water feature, you should assess what features are already there, and how they might affect your plans.

If you are planning a feature that is more complex than a basic hole in the ground filled with water, then it would be wise to produce a scale drawing or plan of the area. This should include all of the garden's 'fixtures and fittings': the house; greenhouse/shed; immovable and desirable trees and shrubs; paths and driveways; paving and walling; drains and sewers; electricity poles; and so on. Consider also whether you will want to extend your home at some stage in the future; you do not want to install a major water feature only to dig it out 18 months later when a home extension is built.

It is possible that there are some items in the above list that can be altered or moved to accommodate your water feature. This becomes a matter of preference, but there is a lot to be said for designing your water feature

Ponds with pumps need ready access to a power supply

into your garden whilst minimizing the overall effort. But the golden rule has to be: do not compromise the garden just to save on effort. If the pond really needs to go where the greenhouse is currently sited, and there is somewhere else for the greenhouse to go, then do it.

Survey

The best way to start a paper plan is to conduct your own 'survey' of the garden. Walk around the house (and any fixed outbuildings) and make a large sketch of the layout, in plan form but not to scale.

A long, flexible measuring tape is useful, and a good starting point is a particular part of the house, say the back door. Measure the distance from the door to your proposed water feature. This gives you a mental picture of distance combined with an actual measurement.

You could even prepare a plan and then move cutouts of different shaped and sized ponds within the layout until you are happy with a particular grouping. Alternatively, there are a number of excellent garden design software packages which will offer you much versatility in drafting a plan.

Lastly, lay a hosepipe on the ground, as an outline to your proposed pond site. Live with this for a few days: you will then be able to make adjustments, and satisfy yourself entirely that it is the best place, size and shape for your water feature.

Aspect

The first thing a gardener usually wants to know when they move to a new home is in which direction the garden faces. In the northern hemisphere, a southerly facing garden gives the least amount of shade; therefore, by default, in the southern hemisphere a northerly facing garden is the least shady.

In addition to the direction, you will need to have knowledge of where the sun shines at different times of the day, and how (and where) the house, any outbuildings, or large trees and shrubs will cast shade.

To reach its full potential, a pond should be positioned where the sun can shine upon it for at least half the day – this does not apply to very hot countries; in places like the Mediterranean and north Africa, some shade is positively beneficial.

Waterlilies only give of their best if they receive six hours or more of sunshine per day, so in the countries of Northern Europe, for example, where the sun does not get very high in the sky, a pond containing them really does need to be in the sunniest position possible.

Specific conditions

Each garden is different, with its own specific, prevailing conditions to take into account. The illustration below is a representation of a 'typical' garden, comprising a number of different elements that usually feature in most gardens. Of course, your own garden may look very different from the one illustrated here, but you will almost certainly need to take the same factors into account when planning your water feature.

KEY

This symbol denotes the shadiest parts of the garden, typically to be found wherever a tree or building casts a shadow.

The yellow line denotes the sunniest area of the garden. The sun will shine on both sides of the line for most of the day.

This blue arrow denotes the direction of wind. In this case, the wind swirls over the top of the fence and down the garden.

This green arrow denotes a gradient in the garden. In this case, the floor slopes diagonally from one end to another.

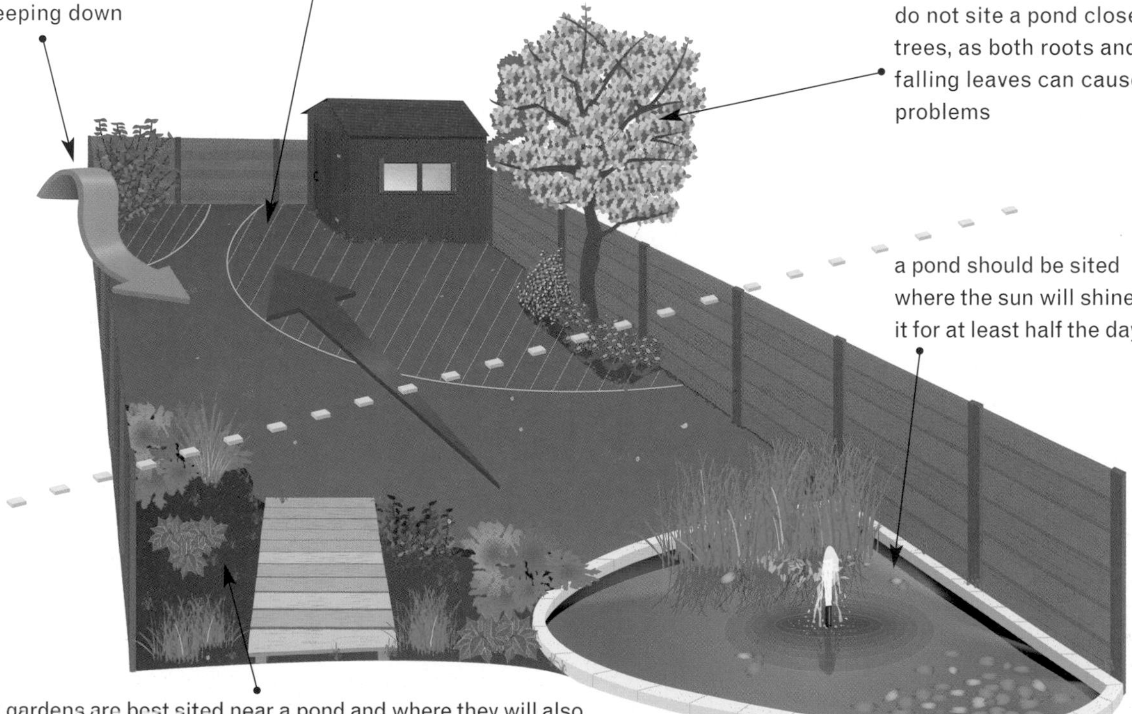

the prevailing wind can cause problems. Do not site a pond where it will experience eddies caused by wind flowing over the top of a solid barrier and sweeping down

avoid siting a pond in the shade caused by a building

do not site a pond close to trees, as both roots and falling leaves can cause problems

a pond should be sited where the sun will shine on it for at least half the day

bog gardens are best sited near a pond and where they will also receive some shade during the day, such as by a fence, as here

Pond Styles

A small water feature could be a pebble fountain or a half-barrel with a trickling urn, both of which are ideal accompaniments to a tiny town garden or patio area. Garden ponds, perhaps 1–2m (3–6ft) across, are what most gardeners would like to create, and these can be wonderful to observe and nurture. At the top end of the scale you could opt for a lake or a large bog garden – if there is the room in your garden.

This diversity of choice illustrates the versatility and adaptability of water. Whatever your choice of design and style for your pond, be aware that it should not be too complex, with too many niches, nooks and crannies. These can be a real problem to construct, and then look over-fussy when completed. When in doubt, always opt for the simple approach – straightforward, simple shapes are usually more attractive than awkward, complex designs.

Formal ponds add symmetry to a garden – though they need not always be this large!

Formal

Formal ponds are either circular, oval or have straight lines, in the form of a square, rectangle or some other geometric shape. Formal ponds are particularly suitable where space is limited. They look best in more formal surroundings, such as near the house, or in conjunction with other features such as straight paths and patios. They can also be raised or sunken, which can add another attractive dimension to the garden.

For most of us, the perfect pond is one in which there is some form of moving water. It may be the trickle of a little fountain, or a big gusher with a larger water feature. Formal ponds lend themselves to fountains and waterfalls (where there is free-falling water, rather than the more informal 'cascade', in which case the water tumbles over rocks).

Informal

By contrast, informal ponds are irregular in shape. They may have soft, sweeping curves with few, if any, straight lines or sharp angles. This type of design looks at its best in a garden planted in a relaxed way – a sort of cottage garden, with flowers of all sizes and colours. If you like lots of plants, an informal style of pond would suit you best. For example, a bog garden can be created as 'an extension' of the pond, and makes a perfect transition between pond and garden.

A still-water pond is the most basic type of pond, with no 'sophisticated' appeal, like a fountain or waterfall, and no mechanical filtration using pumps. This may sound rather boring, yet in many cases it is to be preferred if you wish to keep fish and grow many types of aquatic plant – especially waterlilies, which hate too much moving water around their stems and leaves.

Fish or 'mixed' ponds

'Fish pond' is the accepted term, but perhaps 'mixed pond' would be better, for although a selection of fish may be kept in it, you would inevitably find plants and pondweed, insect life and very probably amphibious life such as toads, frogs and newts in such a pond.

Regardless of the eventual constituent parts of a pond, it is the keeping of fish that many gardeners enjoy. The colours, general visual interest and serenity that fish can bring to a scene are unequalled. The only fixed rules about keeping fish in an outdoor pond are (a) that the types of fish kept should be fully hardy and not 'tender exotics' which would come to harm during a cold

DEPTH AND AREA

Wherever it is sited, and whatever style you adopt for it, your pond should be 45cm (18in) or more deep at some point, to prevent the water freezing completely in winter. If the surface area is 2.4m² (50sq ft) or more, and if you plan to have various types of fish, then a depth of 60cm (2ft) is better. For large ponds of several hundred sq ft, a depth of 75cm (30in) is desirable.

For a decent-sized pond, which can be expected to stay clear, you should aim for a water surface of at least 2.1m² (40sq ft). The ideal ecological balance would be achieved by at least a third of the pond surface being covered in plants.

winter, and (b) that the amount and size of the fish you introduce depends on the dimensions of the pond, or more accurately, the volume of water in the pond.

Wildlife ponds

Surveys have revealed that as many as 86% of people who own a garden pond maintain that their main reason for having a pond is to 'watch and encourage wildlife'. They also agreed that informal ponds make the best environments for aquatic wildlife.

In theory, a true wildlife pond would be one that is built entirely from natural materials and contains only plants and animals native to the area. In reality, however, these preconditions are either difficult or impossible to recreate and so most wildlife ponds are artificial havens. And havens they are, for the hundreds of species that will be attracted to the pond, will themselves attract other non-aquatic animals, such as birds, bees, butterflies, hedgehogs, foxes and even badgers.

Raised ponds

Any raised feature in an otherwise flat garden will help to add interest, but one that contains water is always special. Patio ponds are often raised so that you can sit on the edge and appreciate the pond life at close quarters. It may also be the only way of having a pond if, for some reason, the ground cannot be excavated. For example, where a very deep pond

is required (such as for keeping koi), then elevating it to a raised position would mean less excavation, and so reduce the overall cost, which could be huge.

A raised pond can also be a disincentive to marauding creatures – predominately cats and herons, which can mercilessly decimate a collection of fish.

Graduated ponds

A sandy, muddy or stony 'beach', along one edge of a largish pond, can be quite eye-catching. It will set the scene for a completely different range of plants, and will be a wonderful attraction for wildlife. Boulders, pebbles and even shells can be introduced to give the effect of the foreshore.

The only negative aspect to having a home-made freshwater 'beach' is that algae might grow in the shallow water – something which rarely happens in constantly washed seawater pools.

Pond Materials

Ponds need to be watertight and, within reason, it does not matter how this is achieved. When it comes to the material used to form the base and sides of your pond, there are three main options:

• Preformed rigid glass fibre or plastic liners
• Flexible polythene, PVC and butyl liners
• Concrete

Advantages and disadvantages

As always in gardening, things are never straightforward. Whereas a flexible liner is the ideal solution for one gardener, another will prefer the concrete option. The following three areas will need to considered before you make your choice.

A preformed rigid glass fibre cascade

Cost

The question of comparative costs is probably the first thing you would want to investigate. However, the price of liner for a pond of a given size is very similar, whether you opt for the pre-formed type or flexible sheeting.

The cost of liners will vary according to where you buy them. For example, a liner bought from a high-quality garden centre in an 'up market' neighbourhood will, almost certainly, cost more than the same product if bought from a town market or via a mail order supplier.

Both flexible and pre-formed pond liners come in various grades of thickness, and this, too, complicates any price comparison.

In reality, after all variables are taken into account, there is little difference in cost between the two types of liner.

Ease of installation

In its simplest form, making a pond with a flexible liner involves digging a hole, placing the liner into it, and then filling it with water. Pond making could not be simpler.

However, without attention paid to trimming, folding, tucking and, possibly, glueing, the end result may be less than satisfactory.

On the other hand, a pre-formed pond freshly delivered from the retailer is ready to be sunk into a hole in its chosen place. However, the hole needs to be dug to exactly the right shape and size, and kept perfectly level. This is easier said than done.

Both types of liner need underlay or soft backing to prevent large stones from penetrating the material once the pond has been filled with water. Indeed, the quality of the soil, and the ease with which you can create a hole in it, may be the single determining factor.

One might conclude that a simple, shaped pre-formed liner would be better for a small square or round formal pond, and that a flexible liner is better if you want a large, informal pond. Ultimately, however, the desired shape of pond will have the main bearing on the liner that you select, and you may find that the conditions which prevail in your own garden are a particular consideration.

Ease of maintenance

On-going maintenance is usually of concern to pond owners who are planning to live with the same garden for at least 10 years.

Ponds made of concrete do tend to be the most labour-intensive in terms of on-going maintenance. Ground movement can create cracks, and old concrete can become brittle. Repairing kits and sealants are expensive.

Cheap-grade flexible liners, when exposed to sunlight, will degrade in time. Liners with a guarantee of 10 years or more should be sought (even better are those with a 35 year guarantee).

Pre-formed glass fibre or moulded plastic ponds are extremely rigid, and usually thick enough to repel knocks and grazes. However, a badly placed boulder set underneath the filled pond can do more damage to a pre-formed liner than to a flexible one.

Rigid & Moulded Plastic Liners

What to look for

Rigid moulded liners made from vacuum-formed plastic are the cheapest. They are also relatively easy to install, and many people like them because the shape is predetermined. They usually come with built-in shelves. Longer-lasting PVC-based and rubberized compounds are available, and moulded fibreglass is better still, but not so easy to find, and is more expensive when you do.

How to buy

Garden centres usually offer a selection of pre-formed pond liners. The larger centres, or specialist aquatic and water garden retailers, will offer a better selection.

There are also a number of very good mail order companies specializing in water gardening products. Whereas these companies generally have a selection of pre-formed ponds, bear in mind that you will almost certainly have to pay for delivery.

It is important that you do not simply buy the first rigid liner you find. It will pay you to shop around until you find one that perfectly suits your requirements. Remember, too, that rigid and moulded liners always look bigger when stood on end, or even sitting on the surface of the ground, and it is not unusual for the prospective water gardener to be disappointed that the pond, when in situ, appears to be smaller than originally envisaged. So, be aware of this and, if the space allows, over-estimate the size of unit that you require. If you are intending to keep fish, check that the unit is of an adequate size, and deep enough (see the panel on page 11). Another thing to bear in mind when buying a rigid liner is to check that the moulded shelves that are intended for marginal plants are wide enough to accommodate the planting baskets properly.

Installing a rigid pond liner

With this type of pond, the hole into which the unit will sit is crucially important. If your chosen pond is a regular or symmetrically shaped unit (square, circle, rectangle, oval, etc.), turn it upside down, and position it so that it is directly over the precise place you want the finished

A selection of rigid and moulded plastic pond liners

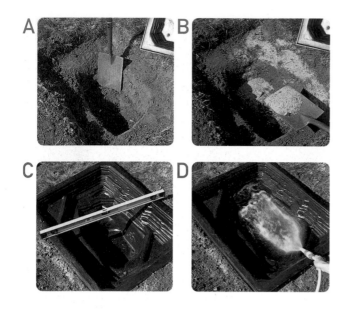

Now check the hole thoroughly, removing any large or sharp stones. Compact the soil, and then spread a 5cm (2in) layer of builder's sand on to the base [B]. Lower the pond gently into position, and add or take away sand until you are happy with the level.

Woven fibre underlay, similar to carpet underlay but thicker, is available and can be used with pre-formed liners. They are, however, more ideally suited for use with flexible liners.

Keep checking with the spirit level [C]. If you have measured correctly, the lip of the pond should end up lying just below ground level.

Next comes the satisfying bit – running water into the unit for the first time. But don't fill the whole pond. Run just a few inches into the bottom to stabilize the unit, and to bed the bottom of it on to the sand base [D].

Then fill in some of the larger gaps around the edge of the pond unit with sieved soil or builder's sand. To backfill, pour the sand or soil into the space and then ram it down with a large piece of wood. This will help to ensure that there are no air pockets.

Add more water and backfill as you go. By doing the filling and backfilling at the same time, you are exerting even pressure on to the sides of the unit – front and back – and so avoiding buckling of the walls.

Fill to about 10cm (4in) from the lip of the pond. This will allow you room to complete your job, which may be to plant perennials or bog plants along the edge of the pond, or to lay paving stones.

pond to be. Depending on the shape and size of the unit, this may or may not be a two-person job.

With a stick, spade, or handfuls of sand, mark an outline right around the rim of the unit, but bringing the mark out from the edge by about 15cm (6in). This extra space will allow for miscalculations in digging and, just as importantly, will permit backfilling later with soft soil or sand.

If your chosen pond is not symmetrical, but of an informal style (such as the most popular 'kidney-shaped' style), then upturning and marking out as described above will not work. Instead, place it upright over its intended position, and level it out with supports. Insert stakes or canes vertically into the ground at intervals all the way around the unit.

Then remove the unit, and measure the depth and size of any shelves that are moulded in to it. Now with your spade, dig a level, flat-bottomed hole as marked out, but only dig to a depth that is just a little deeper than the level of the first shelf. Rake over the bottom of the hole, and then stand the pond unit inside the hole and press down so that once it is removed again you will see that the deeper section of the unit has left an impression.

Remove the unit again and excavate the newly marked section down to about 10cm (4in) below where the bottom of the pond will be [A]. Always check that the pond is sitting horizontally by using a straight-edged board and a spirit level. Check in six or seven directions so that the hole is being dug with a level base – there is little that is worse than a lopsided pond. Water will always find its level, even if the pond is not, and it will look hideous.

Flexible UPVC Liners

These are basically lengths of waterproof sheeting, enabling you to build a pond of any shape or size. More planning is required for this type of pond, and calculating the amount of liner you need is not always easy.

This pond-lining material is ideal for informal schemes, since the sheeting will fit most shapes and contours, albeit with varying amounts of creasing. Many raised ponds, which at first appearance may seem to be constructed entirely of bricks or concrete, are actually lined inside.

What to look for

The best reliability comes with rubber sheeting known as butyl, but PVC and LDPE (low-density polyethylene) sheets are also to be recommended. Buy lengths with a ten or more year guarantee. Polythene is common at the cheaper end of the scale, but it lacks pliability and becomes brittle after prolonged exposure to sunlight. It is best to avoid these.

Finally there are 'geotextile' liners, which are rubber-based liners impregnated with sodium mentonite (clay). These are self-healing liners in that, should they sustain a minor puncture, the bentonite will plug the hole.

Ideally dig holes for lined ponds with 20-degree angled sides

---

FLEXIBLE LINERS: KEEP IT SIMPLE

When laying flexible liners, it is always better to keep to gentle curves and simple shapes. Avoid sharp corners and fussiness. Both gently sloping and straight vertical sides can also cause problems, so it is better to aim for 20-degree sides.

Ensure that you choose a weight and thickness of liner suited to your needs

How to buy

Most garden centres and some large DIY stores offer a selection of flexible liners. Specialist aquatic and water garden retailers will offer a better selection and there are also a number of very good mail order companies specializing in water gardening products. Whereas these companies generally have a selection of liners in predetermined sizes, you will need to add the delivery charge to your costs.

Installing a flexible UPVC liner

Before you dig the hole for the pond, go around the outside of the proposed pond site, removing a thin layer of turf or topsoil, about 45cm (18in) wide, with a spade. This strip will eventually form the edge of the pond, onto which the flexible liner will overlap, and over which the pond edging – paving slabs, bricks, etc. – will be placed.

Then dig the rest of the hole. With this type of pond the sides can slope to almost any angle from 70 to 0 degrees (that is, a gently sloping pond or home-made 'beach'). The shallower the slope, the better it is for wildlife – 20

A

B

C

thicknesses are so small that your excavation will not need to be adjusted to accommodate them.

Remove any sharp stones or boulders and position the underlay. If you are using sand, dampen it so that it stays in place. If you are using carpet or felt, press it down firmly. It is especially important to run this underlay over any sharp corners, such as that caused by a reinforced back wall of bricks or blocks.

Installing the liner is not difficult. The easiest way to do this is to mould the liner into the excavation, smoothing out as many creases as you can. Then run a hose into the deepest part, adjusting any folds that occur as it fills [B].

Once the pond is full of water, trim the edges of the liner, leaving sufficient width all around to form a good overlap [C].

Before you start with your flexible liner you should always make a good estimate of the amount you need (see box below). Fortunately, shortfalls can be remedied. Water pressure is usually sufficient to hold two overlapping sheets of liner in place. If the bottom of the pond is sloping, the section of liner on the higher level should overlap the one downstream of it. A thin layer of mortar can be used to 'glue' down the overlap.

Finally, cover the overlapping edge of the liner with the materials you have selected for your pond edging [D].

degrees is best. Shape the sides of the hole [A] and the shelves as you dig down, allowing enough width – 30cm (12in) minimum – for standing planted aquatic baskets if these are required.

If your soil is very sandy or loose, it would be advisable to install a supporting back wall to the top shelf, to prevent damage to the edge once the pond is in use. This can be done by lining the back of the shelf with brick or building blocks, cementing them in place.

As excavation proceeds, keep checking with a spirit level to ensure that any shelves are horizontal. It is not so important for the bottom of the pond to be absolutely level, unless you want to place planted containers there.

Prior to laying the butyl or rubber liner, you should install 'underlay'. This could be in the form of a layer of builder's sand some 5cm (2in) thick, so the excavation should be deeper by this amount to accommodate it. Pre-made underlays consist of strips of old carpet, or proprietary underlay felt; with either of these, the

D

FLEXIBLE LINER: CALCULATING THE AMOUNT

When digging a hole for your pond, you can make it any shape you like, but accurately calculating the amount of liner required can be a nightmare. Use this simple formula for the best way to calculate the amount of liner required:

Length of sheet required = pond length plus 2 x pond depth, plus an extra 60cm (2ft)

Width of sheet required = pond width plus 2 x pond depth, plus an extra 60cm (2ft)

Concrete Ponds

Making a pond from poured concrete was once very common, but today you are more likely to come across pre-cast blocks built to form the frame of the pond, after which a flexible liner is used to hold the water.

Making a satisfactory pond from poured concrete takes a great deal of skill, time and hard labour! Achieving the right mix, applying it correctly and keeping it workable are tasks that many beginners get badly wrong. Yet, properly designed and constructed, a concrete pond can be extremely elegant and have an air of permanence unequalled by other materials.

A great deal of fairly strenuous work is involved in creating a pond in concrete. You will need to mix the sand and cement and then transport barrowsful of it to and fro. It also takes weeks to construct a concrete pond, rather than the mere day or two required for the alternative methods. However, what makes concrete a realistic option is its longevity: if a concrete pond is made well, it will almost certainly outlast either rigid ponds or those constructed with flexible liners.

Excavation and lining

Mark out and dig the hole, making it about 15cm (6in) deeper and wider than the finished desired size. Shape any shelves and firm the surface of the soil so that there are few loose fragments. Ensure that the sides are no steeper than 45 degrees – otherwise you will not be able to prevent the wet concrete from sliding to the bottom of the slope.

If your garden soil is heavy clay then you may have noticed that in the summer it will become dry, and with it there will be cracking. It effectively 'shrinks'. It would not be good for the concrete to be in regular contact with a soil that expands and shrinks in this way, so you should line the hole with a 7cm (3in) layer of moist builder's sand. If you live on a sandy soil, this stage can be ignored.

Mixing and laying the base

The hole should then be lined with a 5cm (2in) thick base layer of concrete. Although it is possible to build the whole pond using one strength of concrete, a far stronger and more durable pond will be created if you adjust the ratios. Ideally, there should be three stages. The first stage – the base layer – should be mixed to the following recipe: 7 parts 15mm (⅝in) gravel; 3 parts builder's sand; 1 part cement. Measure the ingredients dry, with a shovel or bucket.

Always mix the concrete as near to the pond site as possible, on a hard surface such as paving or a large

Concrete is a good medium for a large, ornamental pond with a clear water effect

board. The concrete consistency should be stiff, but moist. Plan the job so that each layer is completed in a day, with overnight hardening and drying. Weak joints may be created if you add a new layer to a previous layer that has not set properly.

An hour or so after you have finished laying the base, use a stiff broom to brush the drying surface, and so create a rough key for the next layer. Leave the concrete to dry overnight.

Strengthening with wire

Next day, cover the base layer with 5cm (2in) mesh wire netting. This will reinforce the concrete. Overlap the strips of wire by about 10cm (4in) and tread it into place, using your feet to mould it into the contours of the pond.

Then mix and lay another lining of concrete, but this time make it about 10cm (4in) thick, and made to the following recipe: 3 parts 15mm (¾in) gravel; 2 parts builder's sand; 1 part cement, plus optional waterproofing agent to bind the mixture together. Smooth the edges with a builder's trowel, and leave it to set for a couple of weeks. Protect the surface from strong sunlight (with sacking or horticultural fleece). In really hot weather it is advisable to damp it down with a watering can.

After the two weeks have passed, spread a 5cm (2in) thick final layer of concrete over the whole area. This should be made to the following recipe: 4 parts builder's sand; 1 part cement, plus waterproofing agent. Leave to set for a further couple of weeks.

Primers and sealants

Once the final layer of concrete has set hard, coat it with a waterproofing primer and sealant, and leave it to dry. Sweep the interior of the pond and flush out all debris prior to filling with water. This will also help initially to reduce the amount of lime in the water.

If a concrete pond has been well sealed, no toxins should leach out from the concrete. To be sure, use a pH test kit after filling the pond with water to check on its acidity/alkalinity levels. If the resultant level is over pH8.5, this indicates a high lime content. Neutralize it by adding potassium permanganate, which will initially turn the water a light pinkish colour, and leave it for a few days. Empty the pond, rinse it thoroughly, refill and re-test. Once you are happy with the pH level, do not be tempted to introduce fish – this should be delayed for a further four to six weeks. Installing clumps of oxygenating plants at this stage would, however, be a good idea.

Raised Ponds

Patio ponds are often raised so that you can sit on the edge and appreciate the pond life at close quarters. A raised pond may also be the only way of having a water feature if, for some reason, the ground cannot be excavated. If a very deep pond is required (such as for keeping koi), then elevating it would mean less excavation, and would also reduce the overall cost, which could be huge.

Setting the foundations

Raised ponds need low walls to support the weight and volume of water. Good, deep foundations are crucial. Use wooden pegs hammered into the ground and a line to mark out the eventual position of the wall. A 60cm (2ft) deep trench needs to be dug. This will allow for 45cm (18in) of concrete for the main foundation, and a further 15cm (6in) for the first course of bricks to remain below ground level. The trench should be about twice as wide as the width of the wall it will support.

Pour a concrete mix in to the trench. Alternatively, use a modern, ready-to-use dry mix that is poured into the trench and then packed down, smoothed off and watered. It will set rock hard within half an hour. The final level should be at just the right height for the first course of bricks or blocks. Leave to dry overnight.

Building the walls

Most garden walls are built with modern lightweight blocks that are cheaper than bricks and have superseded the previously used 'breeze' blocks made from expensive imported blown volcanic clay. If you're building a small wall, ordinary bricks will be suitable.

Unless there is a designed curve, use pegs and a builder's line to mark out the position of the 'face' of the wall – that is the side of the wall that will be most visible.

Mix your mortar: one part cement to six parts soft sand (or ready-made mixes are available from large DIY stores). Begin by trowelling a 1cm (½in) layer of mortar on to the footing. Then, using your line as a guide, and checking every so often with a spirit level, start bedding in the bricks.

Lay brick after brick, course after course, but after about six courses you will need to take a step back and start cleaning up the mortar, which should be stiff enough to work without all coming out from between the joints. Use a jointing iron to smooth a nice clean finish between each course. Then brush off the small blobs of semi-dry mortar.

Installing a flexible liner

By far the best option when creating a raised pond is to use a flexible liner. The method of laying it will vary according to the overall design and the materials used. Some may wish to build the outer walls of the raised pond and simply lay the liner along the bottom and up the sides. Others may like to build another wall of bricks or blocks to sandwich the liner between. This gives extra durability to the liner, and means that it will always be hidden from view.

A raised pond is a good option to choose when the ground is difficult to excavate

Clay-based Ponds

The earliest ornamental ponds were made from puddled clay, and although this method is still practised today, it tends mainly to be used for larger – even municipal – ponds. The excavated hole was first lined with soot – to deter worms, which would otherwise burrow into the clay and cause leakage. The surface was then plastered with wet clay. Today, easy-to-lay mats that are impregnated with clay are perhaps the better option for back garden ponds.

Natural site and soil

Lining an informal pond with a layer of compacted clay on gently sloping sides gives the impression of an entirely natural pond.

If the normal garden soil is not suitable for moulding in this way, clay may be bought in. Local clay is usually available at a modest price; importing clay from far away, however, is expensive. If the existing soil is suitable, then once the hole has been dug, the base and sides must be well compacted to make it watertight. Trampling over a small area is usually sufficient; larger ponds can be compacted with vibrating plate machines hired in for the job. Remove all large stones, especially sharp ones, as well as large roots. At this stage the soot should be applied.

Building layers

The hole then needs to be lined with a thick, well-compacted layer of clay. This is called 'clay-puddling'. It is best to build up several thin layers; on lighter, sandier soils the eventual thickness should be at least 15cm (6in).

Either plaster the clay on by hand, or with a flat piece of wood to act rather like a plasterer's trowel. Make sure you compact it thoroughly.

Keep the clay wet at all times; as you work, dip your hands into water regularly. As areas are completed,

add a 10cm (4in) layer of good topsoil to the clay layer and then slowly fill with water

remove all sharp stones from the base of the hole, and dust the base with soot to deter worms

cover them in damp hessian sacking until you are ready to fill the pond.

Once the puddling is complete, add a 10cm (4in) layer of topsoil to the base of the pond, and slowly fill the pond with water, from a gently seeping hosepipe laid in the base of the excavated ground.

CROSS SECTION OF CLAY LINED POND
Clay lined ponds should be well maintained and topped up with water so that the clay does not dry out and crack. Avoid growing trees and shrubs nearby.

lining the gently sloping sides of the pond with compacted clay gives a natural appearance

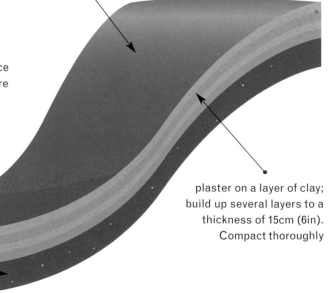

plaster on a layer of clay; build up several layers to a thickness of 15cm (6in). Compact thoroughly

Water Garden Features

If you are short of space in your garden and do not really have room for a pond, you could consider either purchasing or building a water feature. A wide range of different containers, waterfalls, fountains and other devices are now available from good garden centres and DIY stores, or you could create something to your own design.

Water Gardens in Containers

Small water features which do not require an actual pond were once rare to see; today they sell in their millions and can be bought as manufactured items, or made up at home. A small water feature can be anything from a wall-mounted ornate reservoir that is little more than a glorified bird bath, through to wooden barrels, Japanese bamboo bird- and deer-scarers and old kitchen sinks, to more sophisticated pebble and millstone fountains. These can be fairly inexpensive, quick to install, stunning to look at and a marvellous talking point. On the downside, the small size of these features means that the range of fish or plants you can keep in them – should you choose to do so – is limited. Additionally, shade is required for part of the day, as otherwise in very hot weather the water temperature will rise to dangerous levels for the waterlife. Regular checks must also be made to replenish water levels. (See also pages 148–153.)

Types of container

Pots, urns, tubs, baths, vases – and of course the ubiquitous water barrel – whether they are self-contained units or linked to a larger pond, really add a different dimension to the garden. Any container that can hold water is a potential above-ground pond. It should, of course, be ornamental, decorative and watertight.

Siting contained water features

These containers can be placed almost anywhere in the garden, but because they are relatively small compared to a whole pond, it makes sense to site them in proximity to where people are going to sit or spend an amount of time. Placed to brighten up a dull corner, they can make perfect alternatives to containers of plants.

This wooden barrel with a simple built-in pump and spout makes an effective feature for a small space

The most important factor to consider when placing a container feature in your garden is light, particularly if you are anticipating growing flowering water plants like waterlilies. Do not site the water container in a dark corner; however, it should also not be positioned in full sun for the hottest part of the year, as otherwise evaporation will become a problem.

Another factor to consider is that of running power out to the container, as you will almost certainly require the water to be moved around with the aid of a pump.

LINING A WOODEN CONTAINER

Many metal, plastic or ceramic containers will already be watertight, but water barrels – or more correctly half-barrels – might be authentic old style examples made by coopers, and in these there may be gaps between the wooden slats. In this case, you should use a flexible liner to waterproof the barrel.

To both protect the wood, and to ensure that no harmful residues from the wood escape into the water, paint the insides of wooden containers with a recommended aquatic sealant which is plant and fish friendly.

Fountains & Waterfalls

Moving water – whether it is spurting, trickling, cascading or even plummeting – is one of the joys of pond-keeping. Smaller features may include spurting frogs, millstones, lion's heads and even cherubs. Then there are the larger features requiring the movement of a greater water volume, such as streams, waterfalls, long cascades and high-rise fountains.

Fountain design

Apart from conventional spray fountains, you could opt for one of the following:

- **Wall-mounted features** These are usually cast into a block, made from concrete or reconstituted stone. A small pipe feeds water through the back and into the mouth, so this needs to be built into a backing wall behind the feature from the outset. Water pours directly into a pool below.
- **Bubbling stones, millstones and 'boulders'** A strong steel grid – hidden by pebbles – holds a heavy stone fountain over an underground tank of water. A submersible pump pushes water up and through it.
- **Geyser 'foam' jets** These suck in air and mix it with the water to produce a column of foaming water.
- **'Bell' jets** These compress a flow of water from a

> **CASCADES**
>
> Most cascades are modelled along natural lines, but modern and contemporary equivalents, using sheets of glass, stainless steel and wooden channels, are becoming more frequently seen.
>
> A domestic garden cascade can be fairly vertical, with a series of rocks protruding from each other to form the water course. Alternatively, it could be a shallow, nearly level course, where the water will appear more as a stream.
>
> Prefabricated sections are available from most large garden centres. They can be bought as short, self-contained header pools/cascades, or as several units which fit together, to make longer courses.

nozzle, deflecting it outwards to produce a glassy 'mushroom' of water. The pond water must be clean and free of debris.
- **Solar-powered fountains** These are now more efficient, and more widely available. Output is not always as good or as substantial as that in conventional fountains and pumps, but this technology does make it possible to have a modest fountain in a place where it is difficult to run electricity.

Waterfalls

A waterfall can be made to spill gently over a shallow sill, or gush in torrents over a high ledge, depending on its design and construction. If there is no degree of free-falling of water, and instead it is merely tipping and tumbling over rocks, then this is not a waterfall at all, but a 'cascade'.

There are prefabricated, moulded units available to act as the 'header' to a waterfall, and they are simple to install. All you need to worry about is that they are level from side to side, and that the lip protrudes sufficiently over the pond, and at a suitable height, to enable a body of water to fall into the pond rather than on surrounding ground. The hosepipe linking the pump to the header pool should be carefully hidden.

Fountains can be small, such as this little millstone feature

Pond Edging

An established pond can be a thing of beauty in a garden, but it needs an attractive surround to maximize its visual effect. Additionally, there are times when a pond edging can serve a practical purpose – such as deterring children and animals from the water's edge.

Importance of Pond Edging

The pond surround is as important to the overall appearance of the garden as it is to the pond itself. There are many styles of edging from which to choose. It is important for these to be planned at the same time as the pond, because otherwise the end result could be at best incongruous, and at worst, hideous. There are three main factors to consider when edging a pond, as follows.

Decoration

Good pond edging must be decorative. This can take many forms, from paving – both 'straight' and 'crazy' – and decking, to bog gardens and 'beaches'. Whatever style you adopt, there must be a degree of ornamentation. This will include planting, decorative hard landscaping or accessories (such as statues, garden lighting, bird baths, and so on).

Pond netting will repel detritus and deter birds and animals

If you have small children, it is a good idea to fence off your pond

---

LAWN EDGING

The least natural, and most frustrating pond surround of all is one of maintained lawn. It is least natural because it just does not occur in the wild; grass banks run down to highland streams, but the grass is not maintained in any 'ornamental' sense. Maintained lawn is frustrating as a pond edging because at mowing time you will not be able to avoid getting clippings onto the surface of the pond, and netting them off is a tiresome and often difficult or even dangerous activity.

Disguising pipes

Another important aspect of the pond surround is that it must hide a multitude of unsightly paraphernalia. Apart from the edges to flexible liners, the pond edging should also disguise such items as feeder and return hosepipes that come from submersible pumps, as well as the electric cables which power them.

Safety

If young children have access to the pond, some form of barrier is advisable unless you can guarantee a permanent watch over them. These are usually fairly obvious, and can be unsightly. However, install a gaily painted picket-fence, or green, plastic-covered wire hoop fencing, and you overcome the problem of an unattractive appearance. Not only can such barriers stop a child from falling in the pond, they can also prevent cats and herons from getting to your fish.

Creating a 'Beach'

Design benefits

A graduated pond – which you may like to think of as a 'beach' – is perfect for wildlife. It is quite possible that it will occupy at least as much space as the pond itself. Do not be tempted to create the beach all the way around the pond: this will take up a huge amount of space, and might look ugly.

Construction

Ponds with a beach can only really be made with flexible liners (concrete is possible, but is time-consuming and expensive to lay). Start by laying the liner as if for a normal pond. Excavation of the beach area should begin at its farthest point from the pond. Extend the liner from the deepest part of the pond, and slope it upwards towards the 'beach'. The liner should never be nearer to the surface than 25cm (9in). At its extreme edge, bring the liner up against a vertical wall of soil, and trim it as necessary; cover the cut ends with soil or stone. The beach effect is created by adding a 25cm (9in) depth of pebbles, shingle, sand or even mud at the shallow edge, and then less depth as you work your way towards the centre of the pond.

'Muddy beaches'

This type of graduated edge is best for attracting wildlife. Some way along the lined slope, in water about 20cm (8in) deep, build a retaining 'wall' comprising old turves. This wall should be about 15cm (6in) high. To help keep the turves in position, the bottom turf should be longer – perhaps 90cm (3ft) – and draped over the edge.

Fill the area between the turf wall and the vertical part of the liner at the far end with a heavy clay loam. Once the soil is in place, compact it and rake it so that the far end is at the same level as the adjacent garden soil or lawn. Slope the compacted soil gradually downwards until it meets the top of the turf wall. When the pond is then filled, the water level will rise above the turf wall and be absorbed into the compacted soil to form the mud beach.

Sandy beaches

A sandy beach can expand beyond the vertical section of liner. The sand within it will be wet, becoming progressively dryer the further out you go from the pond, whilst the sand outside of the liner will be as damp as the surrounding soil, and will even be bone dry on a hot summer's day. Instead of a turf wall, the retaining wall for a sandy beach should be made from stone, mortared to hold it in place.

This shingle beach leads the eye into the pond and enhances it as a feature

If you want to entertain regularly, it is worth having the decking (and therefore the pond) reasonably close to the house. Be aware that if the decking overhangs the pond, it would be advisable to have some form of balustrade along the exposed edge. Carefully placed trees and large shrubs can offer shade in bright sunshine, and also privacy.

Decking timbers

The early forms of timber used for decking were often untreated, and so the wood rotted or went green and slippery. Today, pressure-treated timbers are used, and often they are cut with many grooves along the length of each timber, to provide a key for foot traffic and so prevent slippage in wet weather.

Constructing the decking from long boards is one option. Decking 'tiles' (pre-made square-framed decks) can be very attractive, particularly in a smaller garden. A country garden can even accommodate a few high quality wooden pallets as rustic decking. These may need some extra fixing, but can be very durable.

Construction

The decking should be constructed in accordance with good carpentry practices, using boards and joists, and supporting members. All pieces should be correctly jointed and secured with galvanized fixings. The joists should be set atop supporting members, such as concrete blocks set on concrete foundations. These may be set on dry land, or under the surface of the water; the crucial matter is to ensure that they are all perfectly level. In the case of underwater supporting members, these can be set onto a thick, flexible liner.

Wooden Decking

The idea of surrounding a pond with wooden decking originated in America, Scandinavia and the Far East, but is now popular all over the world. In recent years manufacturers have emerged to make this a popular and affordable garden feature.

Design benefits

Compared with traditional paving, timber decking blends well with the garden. The decking can be constructed adjacent to the pond, ideally with enough overhang to conceal the liner. This will also give a sense of the water disappearing beneath, perhaps flowing onwards to some other secret location. It is not a good idea for the decking to touch the pond water, as it will rot if left in prolonged contact; allow a gap of 5cm (2in) between the base of the decking and the surface of the pond at its highest level.

Entertaining/lifestyle benefits

Timber decking is consistent with the concept of the garden being a 'living space' – the fabled 'outdoor room', or the equally quoted 'extension of the home'. As a material, wood is warmer than stone paving, and more comfortable underfoot, which lends itself to barefoot traffic, especially in the warmer months.

ROSEWARNE
LEARNING CENTRE

Stone Paving

Paving comes in the form of slabs, tiles, blocks and bricks (often called pavers), and they generally make the best and most clearly defined pond edges, certainly where a formal pond is concerned. The paving style should be chosen to complement nearby hard landscaping, for example, low patio walls. Manufacturers of reconstituted stone materials often design paving and walling materials that complement each other.

Design benefits

Natural and/or artificial stone can make ideal partners for a pond, whether as some kind of paving around the edge, or walling to form the sides, or rock and stone to form the water feature itself. Natural quarried stone is ideal for many gardens, particularly if you want your feature to be sympathetic to the local environment. But most – particularly real slate – can be extremely expensive to buy.

On the other hand, the excellent choice of artificial paving and walling (mostly concrete) can be very realistic, is cheaper, and often simpler to lay.

REGULAR VERSUS CRAZY PAVING

For centuries, straight-edged paving slabs have been the preferred form of paved surround, particularly in the case of formal ponds. They are still popular today, in either natural or reconstituted stone.

In the 1970s, crazy paving became extremely fashionable, and it still has a place in more informal settings. Sandstone is particularly suitable for this style of paving, as it breaks up easily into flat, thin pieces. The trick in achieving a successful area of crazy paving is not just in butting together the irregularly shaped pieces, but also in achieving a level finish, as each piece of stone may have a different depth.

Construction

Paved pond edges need to be supported on well-founded low concrete or block walls. This wall can be set on top of the flexible liner, which is pulled up vertically behind the wall and concreted into place.

Lay the surface slabs flat at first, selecting those which follow the shape of the pond with a reasonably close fit between them. Place some of the larger stones so that they project over the water by about 5cm (2in), to cast a deep shadow line and reflection. Overhanging stones need to be large enough so that they don't topple into the water if you stand too close to the edge.

If too much weight is put onto small overhanging stones, the mortar may not hold them in place. Therefore stones used to overhang should be fairly large, with 80–90% of each stone being firmly fixed onto a mortar bed.

Once you have positioned around 75% of the stones, you are ready to bed them down. Use a bricklayer's trowel to spread a layer of waterproof mortar – 1 part cement to three parts soft sand – about 2.5cm (1in) thick.

Set each stone in position, a short distance from its neighbour. Firm or tap level with a mallet, checking all angles with a spirit level. Then fill the joints and smooth them flush with an old paintbrush.

Most importantly, when working with cement near to a pond, don't drop any into the water, or you'll have to empty and refill the pond before you introduce fish or plants.

Stone paving surrounds are more expensive, but have a permanent, solid quality about them

Running Electricity to Your Pond

If you want to run a fountain or a waterfall in your pond, or you want some garden lighting, you will need to supply power.

The whole subject of electricity and electrical safety must be treated with caution. Electric wiring outdoors is much more likely to get damaged than wiring hidden inside house walls, floors or roofs. Classic examples are cutting through a flex with a hedge trimmer or lawnmower, or digging into (and perhaps through) a buried cable.

Electricity is also dangerous outdoors – especially in and around a pond – because of the close proximity to water (or at least moisture). As we all know, water and electricity do not mix.

To ensure safety with electricity in the UK, installations must comply with the IEE Wiring Regulations (BS7671). Although a professional electrician will be fully familiar with these regulations, if you carry out the installation yourself, for safety it must still comply in every respect. You may find that you are not insured if it doesn't.

Safety RCDs

What makes electricity dangerous to you in the garden is that you could provide a perfect earth connection if you touch a live wire – particularly if you are standing on damp ground – and the short circuit that then passes through you could be fatal.

This is where residual current protection comes in. A residual current device (RCD) monitors the currents flowing in the live and neutral wires of a flex or cable and acts like a switch to cut off the electrical supply if it detects even a tiny difference (perhaps because some of the current is trying to flow through you).

To fit an RCD, unscrew the switch face and lift out the innards of the unit [A] to reveal the cable connection terminals [B]. Feed the cable through the protective rubber flange [C]. Position the socket in place, and mark the fixing points. Using a masonry drill to create the screw holes, fix the unit to the wall with plugs and screws [D]. Connect the conductors to the appropriate terminals, close the face of the unit and switch on the power. RCDs have saved the lives of people who have, for example, cut through the flex of a lawnmower. It is fair to say that an RCD should ALWAYS be used with outside electrics. If in doubt, consult an electrician.

Low voltage garden electric circuits

Much of the electric wiring you will have in or around your pond is likely to be low-voltage. That is, run at a safe 12 or 24 volts from a transformer. Only the transformer needs be connected to mains electricity; the low-voltage cable, which runs to the pond lights or to a low-voltage pond pump, can then be run along the surface of the ground without posing any danger.

Legislation, and therefore manufacturers, err on the side of safety, and in many countries electrical items such as pond lights must be low-voltage: mains-voltage versions are no longer permitted.

Plug sockets should feature protective covers at the very least

Mains voltage garden circuits

Serious pond owners will want to have a permanent outside electric circuit. Unless you are extremely competent, a professional electrician should always install this. Such a circuit should have its cable buried in the ground deep enough to avoid being severed by digging with a spade, and must be protected by rigid PVC conduit.

Electrical wiring

The function of 'fusing' is to protect the wiring, not you. In particular, fusing prevents wiring from overheating and, possibly, causing a fire. A big fuse protects the whole house (and all the circuits); medium-sized fuses protect individual circuits; small fuses protect the flex leading to electrical appliances and, sometimes, tiny fuses within the appliance protect its own wiring.

Underwater lighting highlights plants and creates striking effects

Lighting

Lighting can bring water alive at night, particularly during warm, summer evenings. Interesting effects can be created by using coloured lights to illuminate water descending down a waterfall or cascade, or on the upward and downward flow of a fountain. Modestly priced kits, which often feature different coloured lights, can be bought from most garden centres. Sophisticated versions even change colours with moving discs travelling across the bulbs.

Dry ground floodlighting

Simple lighting can take the form of garden candles and torches, but a strong spotlight directed at a fountain or waterfall, causing the water droplets to sparkle against a dark background, is fairly unbeatable.

Remember that you want the lighting to produce an effect – you do not want to see the source of the light. Therefore try to keep the light fittings as unobtrusive as possible (many are available in matt black for this purpose).

Aquatic lighting

Most of the true pond lights sold in kit form can be detached from the fountain nozzle and holding frame, and used instead as floating illumination. Floating spotlights can be placed beneath decking, or under a bridge, to make the structure appear to float.

Fixed underwater lighting can be directed at waterfalls for an eye-catching display. Use a high-intensity underwater light to illuminate water gushing from a vertical fountain.

DO'S AND DON'TS FOR LIGHTING A WATER FEATURE

- Do use simple white lights above ground. These are more restful than coloured lights, and highlight the natural hues of surrounding flowers and foliage.
- Don't light your pond from above. This will simply show up all the dust and debris floating on the water.
- Do illuminate stepping stones or bridges. Apart from being nice to look at, this is also a safety measure.
- Don't suffer the glare. Place your lighting so that it highlights what you want to see, and does not cause enough glare to blind you.

Pumps

If you want to move water from one place to another, then you need to invest in a pump.

The performance of any pump is affected by water temperature, pipe width and length, any angles in the pipework or connectors and the number of water features connected to the pump. With specific features there are such factors as the intended heights of fountains and falls, and the volume of water. All of these can bring about friction loss, which will affect the 'vertical head' – that is, the maximum height to which the pump can deliver water. For all of these reasons, it is generally advisable to buy a pump that slightly exceeds the maximum amount of flow that your feature(s) will require.

To calculate the right size of pump for your pond, you first need to ascertain the volume of water in your pond or feature (see box). You will need a pump that can circulate a volume equivalent to the total volume in your pond every two hours. All good makes of pump will declare on the packaging the quantity of water that they will move.

Submersible pumps

The most common type of pump is the submersible pump, which sits within the body of water in the pond, attached to a hosepipe which carries the circulated water up and away. Unless a particularly powerful pump

> ### CALCULATING THE VOLUME OF YOUR POND
>
> To determine the volume of water in your pond, measure the length, width and depth of the pond in feet and multiply these together. Multiply the figure by 6.25 to give the volume in gallons.
>
> For a circular pool, measure from the centre to the side and square it: multiply the result by 3.14. Multiply this by the depth of the pool (in feet) and multiply the result by 6.25 for the volume in gallons. This equation is simpler than you think!

is required, for a high waterfall for example, this type of pump is the best option.

Submersible pumps can be relatively cheap – because of mass production – but you get what you pay for, and the cheaper models have less of a life expectancy. Never let a submersible pump run dry, as this will damage the motor.

Surface-only pumps

A pump that is designed to be used on dry land is the surface-only pump. This has the advantage of being extremely powerful, so water can be pumped over large distances, or very high for a spectacular fountain display. It should be housed in a dry, well-ventilated area such as a garage or shed, so as to avoid the problems associated with mixing electricity with water (although there are in fact diesel- and petrol-powered versions). Because surface-only pumps are not submersible, they can be stripped down and repaired more readily. These pumps are, however, relatively expensive. Neither do they come with many of the standard 'extras', such as connectors, strainers, hoses, and so on. These will be necessary components to the finished system, and all add to the cost.

Dual purpose pump systems

This type of pump can be used as either a submersible or a surface pump. Some makes need to be housed at a lower level than the water level, so a separate tank is required. However, these pumps offer the flexibility for you to change your mind about their position and use.

Of course, if you want to operate features such as a waterfall and fountain independently, fitting one pump for each feature will often prove more satisfactory.

Pumps come in a variety of sizes and are powered accordingly

Fountains

Fountains can be a joy in any garden situation (see page 22). They work by drawing water through a pump, and then sending it through to a fountainhead, or nozzle. From here the water is discharged, and can come out in a gently tumbling manner, or fly out in jet-form under high pressure.

The optimum height for a fountain is equal to half the width of the pond; at this height, there will be next to no loss of water through splashing. Fountains with fine sprays will generally lose more water than foaming or bubbling jets.

Jets and nozzles

The dimensions of a fountain's spray depend on the power of the pump and the flow adjuster (the device on the pump designed specifically to control the height and width of spray). For small fountains up to 1.5m (5ft) high, a low voltage pump should be sufficient.

The spray pattern is determined by the size and positions of holes in the nozzle. Standard nozzles are usually connected directly to the outflow pipe on the submersible pump, but adaptors can be obtained to connect more complex nozzles.

Water jets give a pond a delightful extra dimension and create spectacular effects

SAFETY GRILLES

As far as children are concerned, the question of pond safety cannot be overstated. Barriers (see page 23), are one option, as is covering the pond with netting, which can be unsightly.

However, a unique safety grille – called Safapond – is now available. It comprises a number of lightweight but incredibly strong, coated metal support beams fitted across the pond just below the water level, with a number of plastic grids clipped onto the beams. A man can easily stand on the grids and, because they sit just beneath the water surface, they are practically invisible. Visit this website: www.safapond.com

Simple, single sprays are the simplest and least expensive of all fountain sprays. They suit small, unfussy ponds. Bell jet sprays emit from specially designed nozzles that produce a thin, hemispherical film of water. With this type of spray, there is very little surface disturbance when the water lands on the pond surface.

Two- and three-tiered sprays can usually be achieved by altering the design arrangement, and the size of the holes in the nozzle of a single spray fountain. The more ornate the spray, however, the less desirable it becomes in an informal setting. Rotating nozzles can create 'twists' of water spray, and different nozzles can form double domes and columns of water. The number of variations that can be achieved is immense.

Installation

To install a simple fountain, place a pump on an underwater platform in the centre of the pond, using a vertical discharge pipe with a fountain jet. For larger ponds where access to the pump would otherwise be a problem, it would be better to site the pump close to the edge, and use a delivery hose to connect it to the fountainhead. Extending the pond edging out and over the top of the pump can conceal it very effectively.

Waterfalls & Cascades

A good waterfall is a strong statement: it dominates its setting and can easily overwhelm other features. Sadly, it is all too easy to miscalculate waterflow, and you can readily end up with a torrent of water crashing from a wide ledge into a tiny pond, or conversely, a tiny trickle into a huge pond. Both will look anomalous.

Flow rate and 'head'

Before you install a waterfall you need a pump, but in order to use the right size of pump you should know the prospective height of the fall, sometimes referred to as the 'head', and the volume of water it can move (the flow rate, or the amount of water flowing through the system). The manufacturer's details usually quote a flow rate for the pump, and the head that the pump can produce at this flow rate.

Grotto waterfalls

This is where water falls from a fairly high header basin, directly in front of some sort of cavern, which can be easily created with concrete. When completed and

VISUALIZING VOLUMES OF WATER

It is difficult to comprehend water volume, especially when it is cascading over a waterfall. Try this simple test:
Using a hosepipe, fill a 9 litre (2 gal) bucket. Time how long this takes. If it takes, say, 50 seconds, divide 3,600 – the number of seconds in an hour – by 50. Then multiply the result by 9 (the number of litres) to give the litres per hour flow rate. The result is 648 litres (142gal) per hour. Now direct the hosepipe down your waterfall. This flow may be more or less than you actually want, but it serves to give you a rough guide to the sort of flow rate you can create with the right choice of pump.

The stepped effect of a water staircase adds height and extra interest to any pond

established it can be a haven for amphibious wildlife, as well as natural ferns and lichens. Alternatively, by installing the pump and outlet within the recesses of the cavern, and by raising the level of the cavern, you can create the illusion that water is coming out of the cavern and falling into the pond.

Water staircases

Classic Italian and French designers made great use of these. They would create a stone or concrete 'staircase', down which sparkling, silvery water tumbles. This feature works best if there is sufficient water flowing over it, so the size of pump should not be skimped. Disguise the ends of the steps with rocks or plants.

Water Filters

Filters help to turn the water clear and clean. They also enable us to keep a greater number of fish, and they help to keep the fish healthy. Filtration removes debris, and it converts nitrogenous fish waste, toxins caused by rotting plant material and other general detritus, into less harmful substances.

There are three basic methods of filtration: chemical, mechanical and biological.

Chemical filtration

This really comes into its own when a pond and filter are first set up, and the chemical and nitrogenous balance in the water has not been stabilized; in other words, the system is going through the process of 'maturation'. The filter medium – such as zeolite – absorbs ammonia from the water as it passes through. The medium comes in the form of light grey or brown chippings made from hydrated silicates of calcium and aluminium, sometimes with sodium and potassium mixed into them.

Mechanical filtration

This is the 'mechanical' removal of solid waste as the water passes through a suitable medium, such as a sponge, synthetic fibre or even gravel. The trapped solids are then periodically removed from the system by hand (back-flushing into a drain is usually sufficient).

Biological filtration

Biological filters support colonies of aerobic bacteria (which flourish in oxygen-rich conditions). These bacteria

A biological filter unit (left) and compact pond filter (right)

convert toxic ammonia into less harmful substances, and then recycle it – the so-called 'nitrogen cycle':

1 During decomposition, fish waste and other organic debris is converted to ammonia by bacteria and fungi in the pond. This can be injurious to fish.
2 A biological filter will trap larger dirt particles in its first layer of foam (this is purely 'mechanical').
3 Nitrosomonas bacteria contained within the filter then consume the harmful ammonia compounds and convert them to nitrites.
4 Unfortunately, nitrites are just as toxic to the fish. So, the filter also has a population of Nitrobacter bacteria that convert the nitrites into nitrates, which are basically inert to fish but are used by pond plants and algae as a 'fertilizer'.
5 Fish eat the plants and algae, so the cycle is completed.

Water Testing

The slightest changes to the water chemistry of your pond can have major effects on the life in it, and so it makes sense to be able to test the water. Testing kits enable you to check levels of pH, ammonia, nitrate, nitrite and protein. If test results highlight areas for improvement, then you should take action as soon as possible. For optimum water quality there are various treatments for reducing high levels of pH, ammonia, nitrites and nitrates.

Some treatments will cure unsightly sludge, algae or surface foam. In most cases these come in the form of sachets of dry granules that are sprinkled over the pond.

The treatments for clearing cloudy water – generally caused by suspended algae – work by bonding some of the suspended particles, making them heavy enough to either fall to the bottom, or to be removed by filtration.

pH levels

The measure of acidity or alkalinity of a substance is referred to as the pH (percentage hydrogen) value. Acidic water is lower than pH6.5, whereas alkaline water is higher than pH7.5. The figure of pH7 and a little either side of it are referred to as being 'neutral'. Most pond fish require a level between pH6.5–7.5. Levels over pH8.5 can restrict plant growth as well as causing stress to your fish, which can lead to infection and disease.

Ammonia

Even the lowest levels of ammonia stress fish, which makes them susceptible to infection and disease. Any sign of ammonia should be treated as an emergency situation for fish. High levels of ammonia in pond water are caused by over-stocking of fish, or too much detritus (uneaten food, fish waste, decaying plants and even dead insects).

Nitrites and nitrates

If ammonia in the pond is not treated, nitrites and nitrates will form. The former are highly toxic and very dangerous to fish. Whilst the latter are non-toxic, high levels act as suspended nutrients, which leads to the growth of unwanted algae.

Protein

The build-up of animal proteins in the water is usually due to the decomposing remains of food, fish waste and other organisms. These, if left untreated, lead to higher pH levels, a build-up of ammonia, nitrites and nitrates.

Pond life cycle

This flow chart (see right) illustrates how general water quality in a pond changes over time, particularly when influenced by the weather and the actions of pond plants and livestock.

FRESH WATER
We start with 'clean' water – either mains water as used to fill a new pond, or as on-going water at the end of the life cycle. After a period of time, this water will become:

USED WATER
Caused by soil contamination, run-off of minerals from surrounding ground, acid rains and other precipitation, fish waste and an excess of (or uneaten) fish food. If the water is not filtered or treated in any way, this will lead to:

DISEASED WATER
Heterotrophic bacteria, which carry diseases, settle in the water. This can lead to a high level of:

AMMONIA (NH3)
If left unchecked this becomes deadly to fish and other pond life. As ammonia accumulates, beneficial nitrifying bacteria and enzymes break it down into:

NITRITE
This is particularly deadly to fish. However, the bacteria and enzymes continue their good work, eventually oxidizing the nitrite, to form:

NITRATE (PLANT FOODS)

Nitrate – not nitrite – is a form of nitrogen that is generally benign to pond creatures, and when combined with various phosphates that are produced at the same time, is considered to be beneficial to plants

However, an excess of nitrates and phosphates, that cannot be absorbed by plants, will lead to:

OXYGEN & NITROGEN
Healthy aquatic plants repay our attentions by returning these two elements to the atmosphere. In time, moisture in the atmosphere returns to the pond as:

PROBLEMS
In the form of methane gas, blanket weed, algae, lack of night time oxygen, acid water, etc.

RAIN WATER
Rain from the atmosphere fills our ponds as fresh water and tops up our mains supplies, from which we also fill our ponds. The cycle is complete.

Pond Cleaning

The best time of year to empty and dredge a pond, to clean the liner and then to reinstall all the fish and plants, is mid- to late autumn. It is not a good idea to empty a pond during the growing season, when everything should be looking established and colourful. Nor do you want to dredge it in the depths of winter when the water is at its coldest – it would be a miserable job. Early spring is when amphibious creatures are spawning and some fish will have live young, so this is not a good time, either. However, many experts reckon that with a good regime of maintenance, and with the correct filtration, pond cleaning should never become necessary at all.

Ponds made from rigid liners or concrete are most suitable for cleaning and scrubbing; you run the risk of damaging the PVC in flexible lined ponds.

There are a number of mechanical aids available to help us keep our ponds clean and the water clear.

Pond vacuums

An aquatic vacuum cleaner will not turn a cloudy pond into a crystal clear lagoon; however, it does remove the silt, sludge, detritus and potentially toxic substances from the bottom of the pond. Algal growth is reduced, and filter systems are made more efficient, so the water becomes clearer over a period of time. A side benefit is that garden beds and borders may be treated to the 'effluent': a dressing of thick, muddy manure (which hungry or chalky soils will particularly appreciate).

A pond vacuum set comprises a collecting tank with motor unit, 10m (30ft) of cable, a suction hose and nozzles, a discharge hose, extension tubes and a hose end connector.

The unit should be positioned some 2m (6ft) away from the pond edge. Place the end of the discharge hose where the muddy water is to be released when the collecting tank is emptied. Connect the unit to the power supply via an RCD (residual current device) and switch it on.

Guide the nozzle to the bottom of the pond, and move it slowly and evenly to vacuum up the mud. When the collecting tank has been filled to its maximum level, a float valve usually switches off the vacuuming operation automatically.

Pond nets

Removing floating debris is fairly straightforward – an ordinary pond net will often do the trick. Garden centres and DIY stores usually stock a range of pond nets of varying sizes. Remember that it takes time and patience if you are chasing small bits of debris – or plantlets of duckweed – around the pond surface.

Pond scissors

To help you cut through dead or overgrown aquatic plants and pondweed, specially-made pond 'scissors' come on a handle around 115cm (45in) long. These are especially helpful in controlling thick blanket weed, which can smother plants and choke fish if allowed to spread across a pond.

Trim the roots of containerized water plants

Cleaning a pond

It is easier to clean a rigid sided pond than it is one with a flexible liner. With the latter there is always the risk of tearing the material as you walk on it or scrub it vigorously, particularly if the liner is ten years old or more. It can be cleaned, however, and as long as you are careful where you stand and what you do, the process you need to follow is the same as for any kind of pond.

Start by removing any pond plants in containers; these can be put to one side, in a shady part of the garden, and can remain there for two or three days if necessary. Larger plants should then be tackled. Often these will be growing rampantly in the mud at the bottom of the pond. Plants like irises, for example, can become so large that it is impossible for one person to move them. Use a knife to reduce such plants piece by piece, until they are moveable.

When any large amount of plant material is removed from a pond, always check the crown and roots for fish or frogs that have got caught up in it. Blanket weed may be a problem, and it is important to get as much out of the pond as possible, at any time of year.

Next, start to reduce the level of the water. You can bale it out with buckets, but this is a long and tiring job, and the water will end up being thrown around the garden indiscriminately. It is better to attach the end of a hose to a submersible pump (perhaps one that normally operates a waterfall or fountain); the other end of the hose can be directed to specific places in nearby borders.

After half of the water has been removed, stop to catch the livestock. Net out all fish [A], frogs, newts and other large creatures, (insects are best left to fend for themselves). This procedure can be long and drawn out, particularly as you will have stirred up the mud and cannot see the fish easily. However, as there is a much-reduced volume of water, the creatures will be more concentrated together. You will need a degree of patience and dexterity; this one part of the process will seem to take a disproportionately long time.

When you have succeeded in netting the fish, store them in a large, watertight container – such as a plastic dustbin. Do not put the amphibious creatures into the dustbin, unless there is a convenient route out for them – frogs and toads can drown if they are not able to breath air from time to time, and in a deep dustbin they can quickly exhaust themselves trying to stay afloat.

Once all of the livestock has been removed, you can turn the pump on again and empty the rest of the water [B].

There will be a thick sludge in the bottom of the pond. Do not allow this to be sucked up by the pump, as it could do irreparable damage to it. This silt will need to be removed by hand – an old dustpan is useful for scooping it out, rather than a spade or shovel, which might damage the pond. Once the sludge has gone you will be able to clean off the areas of liner that are stained with algae. You need not bother with areas below the waterline, as once the pond is refilled, you will not see them.

At this stage make any repairs to the liner [C]. After you are satisfied that the liner is clean and sound, with no leaks, tears or holes in it, you can refill the pond with clean tapwater, using a hosepipe [D]. Reposition the plants after a day or two, but allow the water to settle for a week or so before you reinstall the fish.

A
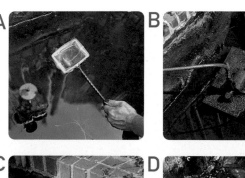
B

C
D

Plants for your Pond

The attraction of a good pond is about far more than just the water. Once the pond is installed you can grow a wonderful selection of aquatic and moisture-loving plants with colourful flowers and foliage that combine to make your pond a truly stunning feature. Not only are aquatic plants immensely ornamental, but they are also essential for creating a balance of nature in your pond, ensuring that it stays healthy with the minimum of maintenance. Aquatic and moisture-loving plants are broadly divided into the following five groups:

• oxygenating plants
• floating aquatics
• flowering aquatics
• marginal plants
• bog garden plants

Oxygenating plants

The reason we have pondweed, or oxygenating plants, in our ponds is because they provide oxygen. This helps to keep the water stable and in good condition. Of all the plants we can add to our ponds, oxygenators are perhaps the least interesting, yet they are almost certainly the most important and should always be included.

Myriophyllum aquaticum is a ubiquitous oxygenating plant

By day, oxygenators convert dissolved carbon dioxide, given off by the fish, into oxygen. They also consume minerals and nutrients that otherwise would be used by opportunist and troublesome algae. A good selection of oxygenating plants will also provide effective cover for all manner of water creatures – protecting fish against marauding herons, and providing spawning grounds for fish as well as amphibious and insectivorous wildlife.

Most garden centres will offer oxygenating plants, normally kept in outside tanks, and generally sold as small bunches of stems linked by a lead weight (which often is not sufficient to carry the bunches to the bottom of the pond where they will root, so it is a good idea to supplement this weight by attaching a pebble to the bunch with an elastic band). You just have to drop these bunches into the pond – you don't need planting baskets or compost. The weights will take the plants down, where they will find their own level (depending on the amount of leaves) and start to grow.

Most oxygenators will grow rapidly, especially in warm summers, and can cause the pond to become congested. You should, therefore, hook out a few bucketsful of excess 'weed', and perhaps do this two or three times during the summer period. This will, curiously, make the weed grow faster, and in turn make it more efficient at filtering and conditioning the water. Carefully check through the foliage as you are removing it. Spread it out by the side of the pond and leave it for a day, so that any creatures caught up in it can crawl back into the water.

Floating aquatics

Floating water plants really are floating plants – they are not anchored by roots, although some do produce a few straggly roots that just dangle in the water. Consequently, they do not require 'planting' in the usual sense.

Aquatic plants such as waterlilies – that have floating leaves but roots which are firmly anchored in pots or in the soil at the bottom of the pond – are discussed in the 'flowering aquatics' section of this book. There are, however, plenty of free-floaters, with no discernible

Eichhornia crassipes is a common floating aquatic plant

Pontaderia cordata is a good flowering aquatic plant

rooting or anchorage, such as water hyacinth (Eichhornia), duckweed (Lemna) and water chestnut.

'Floaters' actually help to maintain clear water; by blocking out some of the sunlight, they effectively check the development of algae – miniscule plant cells that are at their most prolific in well-lit water. As with the oxygenators, floating plants also offer refuge for small aquatic creatures, which can hide in comparative safety in the warmer waters just beneath the surface. These plants tend to die down during late autumn, to survive the winter as dormant 'buds', resting in the mud at the bottom of the pond. In spring, when the weather warms, they burst into life again.

Some floating plants increase their size and number rapidly and, as with the oxygenators, can cause overcrowding in the pond. It is for this reason that there is a restriction in the sale of such plants in some warmer climates, including some of the southern US states, where the winters offer less of a check to their growth.

Flowering aquatics

As we will see later, the distinction between 'flowering aquatics' and 'marginals' is somewhat blurred. It is, of course, perfectly feasible for a flowering aquatic to be grown in the margins of a pond. However, if this position is the natural habitat for such a plant, it will be discussed in

this book in the section covering 'marginals'. It therefore means that plants covered here under the 'flowering aquatics' banner are more at home in the centre of the pond, where the water runs a little deeper. Flowering aquatics grow within the pond, anchored in the mud, or in planting containers. Depending on the plant, they will need a water depth of anything from 30cm (12in) to 1.2m (4ft), or even more in the case of some vigorous species.

Flowering aquatic plants generally produce leaves and flowers that sit on top of the water or rise above it. Waterlilies are the classic flowering water plant, and they typify one of the most important aspects of the group, in that the vigour of their surface spread, and the depth of water to which they are most suited means they must be chosen with great care.

Nymphaea 'Froebelii' has beautiful red flowers

> **TIP**
> Ideally a third to half of the pond's surface should be covered with aquatic plant foliage to prevent sunlight reaching too much of the water, which would encourage the rapid proliferation of green algae.

Marginal plants

Gardeners have argued for years over the true definition of a 'marginal' plant. Some say it is the sort of plant that always has its roots in soil under water. Others say that it is a plant that has its roots in soil that is permanently moist, whilst others even maintain that it is a plant that has its roots growing in soil that is either wet or under water, but which in arid conditions dries out completely.

In reality a 'marginal' should be considered to be any plant that grows at the very edge of the water, regardless of the moisture content of the soil in which it is growing. This means that the marginal plants discussed later will have a wide range of habitat requirements, spanning all soil conditions from being permanently under water to semi-dry. If we are not careful, however, marginal plants will graduate, almost imperceptibly, into bog garden plants.

Bog garden plants

The bog garden, although not a water garden in the purest sense, does have a place in this book. At one end of the bog plant list are those species that like practically to be in the water, and are therefore just slightly removed from the marginals. At the other end there are those plants that require merely a consistently moist soil.

Lobelia cardinalis (marginal plant)

Bog garden plants – sometimes referred to as marsh or poolside plants – generally dislike dry, clay soil that can turn concrete-like in hot, dry weather. Also, they tend not to perform well if they are in a position exposed to high winds and the full strength of the sun all day long. Other than that, they enjoy a wide and varied selection of growing conditions.

Many have colourful flowers and lush, attractive foliage, and they make the perfect transition between pond and garden (as long as the soil is moist).

Grasses and ferns

In this book we have placed these two plant groups into their own category. Both are grown for their foliage, as a foil for other plants and as an attraction in their own right. Between them there are dozens of species that are perfectly at home either in the pond itself (true

Myosotis palustris 'Alba' (bog garden plant)

> **TIP**
>
> Bogs and marshes – which are which? In the natural world, a bog is an area of poorly drained land fed almost entirely from above, in the form of rainwater. A marsh, on the other hand, is a natural wetland fed from below, by the consistent overflowing of rivers and streams, or by the upswell of groundwater.
>
> When we create a bog garden at home, the plants from both types of habitat may be planted.

Festuca glauca 'Golden Toupee' (ornamental grass)

Astilbe 'Venus' (bog garden plant)

informal pond. Some also have attractively variegated or coloured foliage that provides colour and interest from spring to autumn.

Although some members of the grass family grow in the water (rushes and sedges), most of the smaller ornamental species prefer a moist but free-draining soil.

Ferns These shade-loving plants are perfect for the waterside, with their delicate, fresh green leaves (more correctly, 'fronds'). Few plants suggest the prehistoric quite like the fern. They have been around since the age of the dinosaur, which means that they are sturdy, durable and hardy. More often than not they grow in damp places although, it has to be said, a dank atmosphere is as important to them as a wet soil. Indeed, it is quite a common occurrence for the crown and roots of outdoor ferns to rot in consistently wet soil.

aquatics), or in the moist conditions of the bog garden. All have definite characteristics that make them worthy garden plants, but not all gardens are suited to the very idiosyncratic forms the plants take.

Ornamental grasses When browsing through plant catalogues even just a few years ago you would have come across only a mere handful of decorative, ornamental grasses listed. Now that they have become fashionable, there is a bewildering array of species and varieties to choose from, such as the architectural pampas grass and the clump forming smaller forms, like Festuca.

Grasses and grass-like plants are perfect for growing in and around a pond. Their slender stems form elegant vertical clumps that make an ideal contrast to the bold lines of formal ponds, as well as blending and contrasting with other plants in an

Matteuccia struthiopteris (fern)

Choosing & Buying plants

Mid-spring to early summer are the best times to plant up a pond. Consequently, most garden centres will be stocking a wide range of aquatic and moisture-loving plants during this period. Specialist water garden nurseries tend to offer better quality plants, and in a wider range of forms. The prices of plants can vary, too, with specialist centres often selling plants at as much as half the price you would have to pay at a general garden centre. Also, specialist aquatic nurseries can provide customers with good, informed advice; not all general centres can provide this.

Why are spring and early summer the best times to plant? Because the pond water will be sufficiently warm to provide a receptive environment for new plants. These

Inspect plants thoroughly, looking for fresh, healthy growth

plants will have the whole of the summer and autumn to become established before the onset of winter. You can usually buy aquatic plants through until late summer or even autumn, however.

Plants are sold either bare-rooted or grown in containers. The former will be sold to you in plastic bags for planting as soon as you get home. The latter can be left in their containers until you are ready to plant them – but do not let them dry out. Keep them submerged in a tray of water, or in the pond itself.

Recognizing healthy plants

When you purchase aquatic plants, there are certain things you should look out for (sadly, many garden centres and nurseries do not look after their water gardening section as well as they should).

Plants you are considering for purchase should look fresh and healthy with plenty of new growth: avoid any with a lot of dead leaves that could have already spread disease through the entire plant.

Take a good look around the aquatic plant display area. Marginal and deep-water aquatics are usually displayed in trays of water, which should be reasonably clean.

The soil into which aquatic plants are planted must be permanently and consistently moist, so avoid any which have been allowed to dry out.

CHOOSING PLANTS DO'S AND DON'TS

• Do allow new ponds, filled with fresh tap water, to stabilize before planting. It is always a mistake to rush in to planting up a brand new pond. If you have just filled it with tap water, allow it to stand for a few days so that the temperature of the water stabilizes.

• Don't buy poor quality plants. Do not be tempted to buy water plants if the trays they are standing in contain lots of dead or rotting vegetation, weed or algae. This is a sure sign that they have been neglected.

• Do rinse bare root aquatic plants before you plant them or pot them. This is to ensure there are no unwelcome pests (such as leeches) or weeds (such as duckweed) lurking between the leaves or fibrous roots. Duckweed is the main offender here. It is a minuscule, bright green floating plant that tends to sneak in quietly but can soon carpet the entire surface of the pond.

• Don't collect plants from the wild. Firstly, it is likely to be illegal, and second, it is definitely inadvisable, as they may be suffering some disease or virus. The plants may also be harbouring pests, or you might be bringing in to your garden something that is so invasive it will outgrow everything else around the pond.

Plants should be clearly labelled, but do not buy any with badly faded labels – a clear indicator that they have been sitting around for a long time.

Mail order

If you are not happy with your local source of aquatic plants, it is worth considering placing an order with a specialist mail order supplier. You will often find choice and even rare plants with these companies, and many of the plants will have been propagated and grown by them as well. The proprietors are the real water gardening experts, and they are usually happy to impart good advice.

Modern packaging – tough polythene bags and polystyrene packing – and reasonable postage costs mean that the plants generally arrive in good condition, and at an affordable price. It usually compares favourably when you take into account the cost of driving to a garden centre and then paying what can sometimes be inflated prices.

The downside to mail order buying is that you cannot see the quality of the plants before you buy them, which is why it is important for you to use only companies with a good reputation, or which offer a full money-back guarantee for peace of mind.

Before you plant

Once you have got the plants home, you should plant them straight away. If planting is delayed, keep the plant continually moist. Ideally, oxygenators and deep-water plants should be submerged in pondwater or rainwater.

They can survive in this state for two to three weeks, after which time their condition will begin to deteriorate.

Waterlilies, particularly, benefit from a little preparation before planting. If any roots are damaged, or are excessively long, use a sharp knife or pair of secateurs to cut them back to within 5cm (2in) of the tuber. Remove any leaves that have unfurled close to the base, being careful not to damage any new growth. Do not interfere with any young, tightly rolled leaves that are still growing; they will soon reach the water surface.

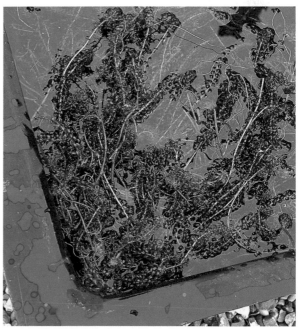

Oxygenating plants are generally displayed and sold in tubs like this one

Installing Plants

Before plastics were commonly used, most pond plants were set directly into the mud in the bottom of the pond. You can, of course, still do this today, and It is usually carried out in large ponds where many plants need to be planted and there is room for them to develop without restraint. It is ideal for a large wildlife pond, where the planting is, for the most part, left to its own devices.

If you want to do this with your own pond, place a layer of soil about 15cm (6in) deep onto the base of the pond liner. Plant directly into this soil and then fill the pond very slowly – even for a period of over a week or more – so as to avoid stirring up the soil with the water.

The main problem with this method is that eventually the plants will grow into each other, with more vigorous varieties smothering their neighbours. You will need to control plants on a regular basis, and weeding a murky pond is not an appealing task.

Soils

Special aquatic composts can be purchased, although ordinary garden soil (sifted to remove twigs, roots and stones), is perfectly acceptable. Use a heavy loam, such as the fertile top layer taken from your pond excavation. Do not add peat, as this will float out into the pond, and do not incorporate garden compost or manure to the soil, as this is far too rich and will pollute the water.

A

B

C
D

Planting in mesh containers

Aquatic plants are best planted in hessian cloth inside plastic mesh containers, as this will both retain the growing medium underwater and will allow the roots of the plant to 'breathe'. The pots come in a range of shapes and sizes. Some retailers now sell plants already in mesh pots, which can be placed directly in the pond.

Planted containers can be positioned in the pond at any desired point, and they can easily be moved when cleaning or maintenance is necessary. A particular advantage of planting individual plants in containers is that each one is shown off at its best.

Do not plant two or more different varieties in the same basket, as plants grow at different rates and to different sizes, so one is almost bound to smother the other(s).

The planting procedure is straightforward. Start by preparing the plants as described on the previous page. When planting up tall marginal plants, place stones in the base of the container for added stability.

Line the plastic mesh container with hessian (sack) cloth [A]. Put a layer of soil in the hessian at the base of the container [B], and then position the plant in it [C], ensuring that its existing soil level is just below the rim. Fill with soil to within 2.5cm (1in) of the top of the container and gently firm the soil.

Add a layer of fine gravel to just below the rim of the pot [D]. This stops soil floating out of the pot, prevents fish from nosing around and stirring up the soil, and provides an attractive finish. Then water the plants thoroughly, using a can with a fine rose-end; soak the compost, which will drive out surplus air.

Trim the roots of water garden plants prior to planting

Setting out the plants

The next thing to do is to place the plant into the pond. Marginal plants can be placed directly in their final positions. Deep water aquatics – plants that need a depth of at least 20cm (8in) in order to grow well (most forms of waterlily come into this category) – need to be 'acclimatized' gradually to their eventual planting position and level. Do this by placing the planted container on a base of bricks – one to four bricks deep, depending on the desired depth. The plants' foliage at this planting stage should be just below the surface of the water. Remember to place some padding under the brick so that the liner does not become damaged. Remove the bricks, layer by layer, over several weeks as the leaves reach the surface.

For larger ponds, suspend plants in the water by running a line of stout string on either side of the basket and anchoring it on both sides of the pond. Gradually

lower the plant as the leaves extend until it reaches its final position, when the string can be removed.

Planting oxygenators

Most oxygenating plants are sold as bunches of unrooted cuttings with a weight at one end. To plant these, simply drop them in to the pond. Sometimes a stone attached to the bunch with an elastic band will help to carry them to the bottom where they will root well. If you wish, you can loosely fill a container with soil. Insert about 7.5cm (3in) of the weighted end of the cuttings into the soil, firm gently, add gravel and place into the pond. These plants should be sited in water that is 30–60cm (12–24in) deep.

Planting a bog garden

The 'bog garden plants' described later in this book are principally herbaceous perennial plants; their distinction from non-bog garden perennials is that they require a consistently moist soil. Cultivation advice is otherwise identical.

Plant them in spring or autumn (container plants are usually available from garden centres all year round). Mesh baskets are not necessary, so plant them directly into the soil. However, take care not to compact the wet soil when walking over it.

Do not add fertilizers or handfuls of rotted or concentrated manures that may run in to the pond water. Finally, plants growing in moist soil usually grow vigorously (think of the giant rhubarb, Gunnera, and ornamental rhubarb, Rheum). Therefore you should give new plants plenty of space in which to spread. Do not overcrowd a bog garden.

Plant Care

Keep pond plants healthy by following a programme of routine maintenance. Remember, however, that aquatic plants are generally more vigorous than conventional garden plants, so you will need to be more attentive. The most important job is the regular removal of dead and dying foliage, as this prevents the build-up of decaying matter and a consequent reduction in water quality.

Cutting back and thinning

Submerged plants can be thinned at any time of year when they become too crowded. Do this little and often, to avoid too much disruption to the water and the mud in the bottom – otherwise algae may result.

Floating plants, such as duckweed (Lemna) and fairy moss (Azolla), can be raked to the side and removed as necessary. Larger floating plants, such as water soldiers (Stratiotes) can have their younger plantlets removed and refloated as required.

Overcrowded plants are more prone to pests and diseases, especially in the summer, so regular division is important. Waterlilies need to be divided when their flowering – either in number or in size, or both – starts to diminish. At this time also their leaves become congested and are held vertically above the water. Dividing them is best done in summer, after flowering, every third or fourth year.

> ### FEEDING
>
> Feeding aquatic and bog garden plants is a simple matter of using tablets or sachets of special slow-release aquatic plant fertilizer. These can be purchased at any good garden centre. During the spring, just push one tablet into the soil of each plant container: one application should last the whole season.
>
> Never apply ordinary garden fertilizers to your pond plants, as there would be a massive release of nutrients into the water which would enable algae to thrive, and could harm fish and wildlife.
>
> Oxygenators and floating aquatics do not need feeding, as they extract sufficient nutrients from the pond water.

Deadheading

As with all other flowering garden plants, removing the faded blooms will lengthen the plants' flowering period. Some plants with single flushes of blooms may, after being deadheaded, produce a second flush. Deadheading also saves the plants' energy (they are not able to produce seed), and in the case of certain potentially invasive plants, it will help to prevent their uncontrolled spread by self-seeding.

Dead flowerheads are usually removed with some of the flower stem attached, using secateurs or pond scissors. You could keep the faded flowerheads of some bog garden perennials – such as astilbes – over part of the winter, as these are quite attractive.

Year-Round Plant Maintenance Guide

Early winter

• Ponds should not be allowed to ice over, because the ice layer prevents oxygen from getting in to the water as well as harmful gases being allowed to escape. But what should you do if your pond does ice over? NEVER crack ice with a hammer. This can be deadly to fish; the shockwaves and reverberation can stun or even kill. Melt a hole with a saucepan full of boiling water. If the ice is more than 1cm (½in) thick, it can take five minutes or more to melt the hole. It will need to be repeated the following day! To prevent ice from forming, install an electric pool heater. It comprises a straight rod element fitted through a wooden or polystyrene float that keeps the heater at surface level. Plug it in to the mains supply and leave it in position whenever hard frost is forecast. Alternatively, keep a section of the pond ice-free by running a fountain or waterfall permanently. The moving water does not become still enough for ice to form.

Mid-winter

• Tender pond plants (such as Eichhornia, the water hyacinth) that are lifted in autumn for storing indoors should be inspected regularly. Sometimes, misting over the tops of the plants is all that they require; otherwise, water them.
• Many people stop feeding fish in winter, while others believe that if the weather is mild and the fish are active, their reserves will be depleted if they do not eat. If the fish are swimming close to the surface, it is a good idea to offer them a sprinkling of food. If they take it they can have a little more; if they decline, then stop.

Late winter

• If you are thinking about making a new pond, or re-shaping or enlarging an existing one, this is a good time to do it. If the work is completed now, you will be able to start planting, and introducing fish in about six weeks, which will bring you nicely into the early to mid-spring season.
• This is the time of year when frogs are mating – and there will be an abundance of frog spawn and tadpoles in your pond as a result. It is important to ensure that any frogs, toads and newts can leave the pond when they need to. Make sure there is a small ramp which these creatures can use to escape.

Early spring

• Remove pond algae as and when you see it. It will only flourish if left unchecked. Also, decaying vegetation will pollute the water and harm the fish.
• With their resistance to infections at its lowest, fish need careful nurturing to restore their normal strength and energy and to improve their health generally in time for the breeding season. Thus, it is important to start feeding them, but do not use too much food or it will contaminate the water.

Other jobs for early spring:
• If you take your submersible pump out of the pond for the winter, now is the time to re-install it
• Test the quality and pH of the water, and make any remedial treatments
• Feed containerized aquatic plants with appropriate pellets; feed established bog garden plants with general fertilizer, but do not allow any run-off to enter the pond
• Lift and divide overgrown marginals
• Plant new plants in the bog garden

In early spring, thin or separate overgrown marginal plants

Mid-spring

• Give bog garden plants a little extra feed now but always use fertilizers with caution near a pond. When there is no wind, sprinkle a handful of fish, blood and bone powder around the base of the plants, rather than spraying liquid feed over them. Some plants may need staking at this time.

Other water garden jobs for mid-spring:
• Introduce new aquatic plants to your pond
• Divide overgrown waterlily clumps
• Make efforts to rid your pond of algae and blanket weed – this is when it can be at its worst
• Check for signs of slugs on bog garden plants and marginals, and treat as appropriate

Late spring

• Tidy the bog garden and remove any dead or diseased foliage. Plants that have finished flowering – such as forget-me-nots – may now be affected by mildew. Cut the affected parts hard back. Deadheading is important. Apart from making the plant less ugly it also removes any places where mould can set in. Never forget that by its nature a bog garden is damp all of the time and botrytis, grey mould and similar diseases may be more troublesome here than elsewhere in the garden.
• If your pond fish have spawned, make sure that the fry have access to a shallow area, safe from the attentions of adult fish that will consider them tasty morsels.

Other water garden jobs for late spring:
• Check for signs of plant pests, such as aphids, and treat as appropriate
• Limit the spread of duckweed at this time, otherwise by the end of summer your pond could be covered

Early summer

• It is surprising how much water can be lost through evaporation on a really hot day, particularly with small features such as water barrels or wall-mounted fountains. Keep the water level topped up regularly; by far the easiest way to do this is with a hose. Make sure that you have a fine-spray attachment, or the pool will be churned up and plants disturbed.

• In hot weather the water becomes comparatively warm and the fish can become lethargic. Feeding should be reduced slightly during these periods.

Other water garden jobs for early summer:
• Thin out overgrown clumps of oxygenators and other fast-growing aquatics
• Weed the bog garden, and apply copious amounts of water during dry spells
• Check and cut back overgrown waterlilies

Mid-summer

• Life in the pond will not come to a grinding halt if you are away, but there are a few things you should do before you go: Ask a neighbour to switch on any aeration device (i.e. a fountain or a waterfall/cascade) for a short while during the period you are away. This will help to oxygenate the water. If you do not have a powered aeration device, tell your neighbour that emptying a bucket of clean water, or running a hosepipe into the pond on muggy days, will do some good. As long as there are plenty of water plants of all kinds in your pond, fish can generally manage well enough for a couple of weeks without supplementary feeding. Block feeders are available for fish in ponds that have few plants.

Other water garden jobs for mid-summer:
• Pond levels may still need topping up in warm weather
• Continue to remove blanket weed and other forms of algae from the pond water

Trim dead and dying material away from plants to keep them healthy

Late summer

- This is when you should start a weekly routine of pulling out dead leaves and stems from your pond, before they sink to the bottom and give off harmful gases.

Your weekly tidying regime should be as follows:

- Cut and clear away any collapsing stems and leaves before they enter the water
- Trim back fading marginal plants by two-thirds
- Leave one or two areas as cover for the various water animals that spend their winter hiding near the banks
- Remove older leaves of waterlilies
- Watch for the two main waterlily pests: aphids and lily beetle. The aphids (blackfly and greenfly) are instantly recognisable. The beetles are brown and small, and they eat holes in and on the edges of the leaves. Fire a jet of water at the leaves to knock the pests in to the water, and remove the worst affected leaves

Other water garden jobs for late summer:

- Divide overgrown marginal plants before the soil and water are too cold for replanting
- Detach young portions of tender aquatic plants (such as the water hyacinth, Eichhornia) for overwintering safely indoors
- Tropical or tender fish that have been enjoying the summer outdoors should be returned to their winter quarters indoors

Early autumn

- Lift and divide any bog garden plants that need it – except the tenderest types, which are better left until spring. Pull apart large clumps and discard the tough older centres, replanting only the more vigorous, outer sections. Leave waterlilies and other fully aquatic species until spring.
- Cut back clumps of marginal species. Leave long stumps, especially if they are a trifle tender and have hollow stems. The accumulation of water within the stem bases, which will freeze during winter, can cause damage and allow rot to penetrate the crown.
- Continue to feed fish regularly, but it is even more important from now on that you make sure they eat all that is given to them. Excess food will drop to the bottom and rot, so scatter a few flakes or pellets and supply more only if the first are completely devoured.

Mid-autumn

- If you prefer to remove the pump and store it over winter, then now is the time to disconnect it. Clean it

A pond vacuum cleaner is a useful device for removing debris

out as best you can, as well as the associated pipe-work.
- Continue to collect leaves from the pond or water feature. The further we go into autumn, the greater the likelihood that ignored leaves will sink to the bottom of the pond, so be prepared to delve into the depths. Try not to disturb the mud too much – many creatures will be hibernating in it.

Other water garden jobs for mid-autumn:

- Continue to remove blanket weed and other forms of pond algae
- As daylight lengths shorten, thin floating plants (such as duckweed and Azolla), to allow as much sunlight on to the pond as possible

Late autumn

- This is a good time for building new ponds (or extensions to existing ones), free from the urgency of spring, the heat and dryness of summer and the cold and inhospitable ground conditions of winter. The weather now is usually warm enough to make the work pleasant, while the risk of prolonged frost is still slight.
- Around now the water in the pond will finally reach 5°C (41°F), the critical point below which all feeding of fish should stop.

Other water garden jobs for late autumn:

- Check your liner (or concrete) above the waterline for cracks and leaks
- Check for slippery paths and paving stones around the edge of the pond – these can be lethal
- Prevent ice forming (see Early winter, page 45)

Propagation

There are various methods which are traditionally employed to propagate water garden plants. Some are easier than others, but all offer a rewarding way of renewing your stock of plants.

Dividing Plants

Spring is a good time to divide plants, as cut surfaces heal more readily during springtime. However, the process of lifting plants out of the water will disturb wildlife that will be breeding at this time of year. Autumn is arguably a better time, giving the plants a sufficient period before winter sets in.

Waterlilies

You can tell that waterlilies have become too big by their leaves: they do not rest flat on the surface of the water. Instead they are bunched up and stand free of the water. This is when the plant should be divided.

Dividing a floating water plant

Dividing ferns

A

B

Take it out of its container and wash off the soil so that the rootstock is clearly visible. This will consist of a main rootstock with smaller side roots coming from it.

C

Using a sharp knife, remove the side roots where they join the main stem, and dust the cut surface with a sulphur-based fungicide to help prevent infection.

Repot each piece of new, healthy root into its own container and cover the surface of the pot with pea shingle.

Floating plants

Floating plants can be lifted from the pond by hand or netted out. Some plants, such as water hyacinth (Eichhornia), produce young plantlets at the sides of the parent plants. During spring these can be detached, even snapped off. Place these young offshoots directly onto the water surface, supporting them with your hand until they have found their floating levels.

Marginals

Marginal plants, including grasses, need dividing in the same way as most other garden herbaceous perennials. They become overcrowded after three years or so, especially if they are grown in containers.

Start by removing the plant from its basket. Cut away any dead or dying material [A]. Smaller plants can be prised apart by hand [B], whilst others will be too big and so you will need to insert two garden forks, back to back, into the plant. Lever the forks apart to split the clump in two. Cut away any extraneous roots [C]. Depending on the size of the original plant, this process can be repeated several times to result in smaller clumps, which can then be replanted. The old centres of original plants should be discarded.

Taking Cuttings

Plants that can be propagated by division offer a fairly 'instant' result in that they can be planted in situ straight away. However, taking cuttings as a means of propagating plants is a much longer process. The resultant 'young plants' are unlikely to survive if they are placed straight into the pond, or planted out.

Before they can be put into their final growing situations, cuttings will need looking after in a protected environment, perhaps under glass. They must be sheltered from the elements, and may need high levels of humidity in order to grow to a sufficient size to survive outdoors.

But taking cuttings is not difficult, and there is a great sense of achievement to be gained by propagating plants this way.

Soft stem cuttings

Some bog garden and marginal plants, including the cardinal flower (*Lobelia cardinalis*), the marsh St John's wort (*Hypericum elodioides*), water mint (*Mentha aquatica*) and brooklime (*Veronica beccabunga* – pictured right) can be propagated by soft stem cuttings.

Using a sharp knife, cut off from the parent plant a healthy, non-flowering shoot about 15cm (6in) long. Carefully strip off the lower leaves and any basal sideshoots. Cut the stem squarely, just below a node (the spot where a leaf had grown).

Dip the bottom cut into some rooting hormone powder or liquid. The cut surface will be sufficiently moist to allow enough of the rooting hormone to stick, but tap off any excess.

Fill a 10cm (4in) square fine mesh aquatic container with aquatic compost. Insert the cutting and firm it in place. Water the cutting in and cover the whole container with a 'tent' made from a clear plastic bag, or

Remove the lower leaves of soft stem cuttings...

...and pot on into a suitable growing medium

place it in a propagator. Keep it there until you can see roots coming out of the bottom of the pot – which should not be much longer than two to three weeks.

Root bud cuttings

Tuberous and rhizomatous plants, such as waterlilies, flowering rush (*Butomus umbellatus*) and some irises, produce tiny new growing points on the rootstock. In mid- to late spring, sections of rootstock containing these buds can be removed from the parent plant, potted up and then grown on to produce a new plant.

Plant each section in its own 7.5cm (3in) or smaller pot, containing finely sifted soil or aquatic compost. Make sure the bud or growing tip is just visible. Then place the pot in a greenhouse or coldframe, in a tray with enough water in it to come over the rim of the pot. As the shoots grow, the young plants will need to be potted on and the water level raised accordingly.

Keep the plants in frost-free conditions over winter, and by the following spring they should be ready for planting out.

> **TIP**
>
> Cutting material needs to be kept fresh and firm, and free from physical damage. Cuttings are at their most vulnerable when they are first cut from the stock plant; soft stem cuttings, in particular, will wilt very quickly. The best time to collect cuttings, especially during summer, is early in the morning, when they are still firm and cool. As soon as it is cut, the material should be placed in a polythene bag to keep it fresh before it is taken indoors for preparation.

Sowing Seeds

Most flowering aquatic and bog garden plants can be grown from seed by amateurs. Plants are likely to take some time to grow to flowering size, so as a method of propagation it is really only practical where a great number of plants are required, or if you want to experiment – and you have lots of patience.

Seeds of most hybridized plants will not grow true to type. Seed sown from plants with variegated leaves, for example, may grow plants with plain green leaves. However, this is not the case with seed from species plants.

Saving seed

A source of free seed is to collect your own, from existing plants. Collect it when ripe, in summer or autumn usually. If it is not going to be sown immediately, it should be stored in small containers of water (yoghurt pots are fine for this).

Some plants, such as the water plantain (*Alisma plantago*), produce prolific amounts of seed, and in the natural habitat this seed will be carried for miles in open streams to achieve distribution of the species.

Seed of aquatic plants generally has a short life span; so sowing within a few weeks of collecting is necessary. For this reason it is not commonplace to find seed merchants offering seed of aquatic plants; this is a very different market to that of the annual and perennial flower seed industry, where dry seed can be stored and packed in sealed and clinical conditions.

If you are collecting seed of perennial bog garden plants, such as Hosta, Astilbe, arum lilies (Zantedeschia) and so on, you can store the seed dry over winter and sow at the appropriate time, usually in late spring.

Sowing techniques

Apart from the type of compost used, and the amounts of water applied to the sown seeds, the technique for sowing aquatic plants is the same as that for garden perennials and annuals.

Fill a pot or seed tray with aquatic compost. Water it and then compress it with a small piece of flat wood. Thinly sow the seeds over the surface; it is crucial that you do not overcrowd them [A].

Then, to retain moisture around the seeds, sieve a thin layer of fine horticultural sand over the surface [B]. For aquatic plants, ideally stand the container in a large tray of water, and keep the water topped up to the level of the compost [C]. Seed of bog garden plants needs to be kept moist, but not saturated.

Place the tray in a light position, such as a greenhouse, until the seeds have germinated. When the seedlings have a pair of true leaves beyond the seed-leaves or 'cotyledons', prick them out into their own small pots – a tray of individual cells is fine for this. Stand the trays in water, or keep the seedlings moist, as before.

Pot the plants on when a good root system has fully developed and you can be sure that they stand a good chance. Overwinter in a frost-free place, planting the young plants out during the following spring.

A

B

C

Ferns

Shade loving ferns have been around since the age of the dinosaur, which means that they are sturdy, durable and hardy. More often than not they grow in damp places although, it has to be said, a dank atmosphere is as important to them as a wet soil. Indeed, it is quite a common occurrence for the crown and roots of outdoor ferns to rot in very wet soil.

Division

Divide congested clumps – as for marginals and herbaceous perennials – in spring. Beware, however, as this is not always an easy job, particularly with the larger forms like the regal fern (osmunda). Chopping off a small portion may be all that is possible.

Fern spores are easy to collect

Collecting and sowing spores

Another way of increasing stock of the fern is to surface-sow ripe spores under glass in autumn or spring. But again, beware! Although ferns produce liberal quantities of spores, many have a very short life, their viability being little more than a few days after ripening.

Collecting the spores is not difficult. When the spore cases (known as sporangia) on the undersides of the leaves (or fronds) begin to turn brown, usually from mid-summer onwards, they are 'ripe'. Cut the frond off the plant and dry it in a paper bag; seal the bag to prevent the spores from escaping.

Sow as quickly as possible. As with normal seed sowing, ordinary seed trays are suitable, however they should be scrupulously clean. Also, the water used to dampen the compost should be boiled and cooled, to avoid the growth of algae, mosses, liverworts and lichens which thrive in the same conditions as the germinated spores.

Fill the container with a 50:50 mix of John Innes seed compost and moss peat. Drench the whole container with water and allow it to drain for half an hour. Sow the spores thinly over the surface of the compost and the cover with a pane of glass, wiping it free of condensation every day.

Keep them out of direct sunlight, in a stable 18°C (65°F). You should see masses of small green growths after about six weeks. When they are big enough, pot them up in the usual way.

Grasses

Overcrowded marginal and bog garden grasses should be divided in autumn or spring. This is the best way to perpetuate variegated and named cultivars. Follow the same rules as for marginals and perennials (page 48).

Species grasses may also be propagated by seed; collect the seed when the flowerhead turns brown, first checking that the individual seeds come away readily. Sow in autumn or spring, and if the former, make sure that seedlings are kept in a frost-free greenhouse over winter. Follow the general advice for sowing (page 50).

Hakonechloa macra 'Aureola' makes a good bog garden grass

Oxygenating Plants

There is only one real reason to have oxygenating plants in your pond... and that is to provide oxygen. This helps to keep the water stable and in good condition. Of all the plants we can add to our ponds, these are perhaps the least interesting. Yet they are almost certainly the most important.

If your pond contains too many fish, or there are not enough plants (particularly the oxygenating type), the water becomes short of dissolved oxygen. This will result in fish either gasping for air at the surface, or lurking at the bottom, utterly disinterested in their food.

Then, if you add outside influences such as a spell of still, sultry weather that warms up the water so it can hold even less dissolved oxygen, and a general lack of water movement, you can very readily end up with some extremely sick fish.

It is not difficult to increase the oxygen level in the water – you can turn on the fountain or waterfall (if you have them), which adds and mixes oxygen as the water turns and tumbles. However, if you have a still pond, the simplest thing to do is to make sure you have a plentiful and permanent supply of oxygenating plants. They are cheap to buy, and are perhaps the easiest plants to grow and look after of any in the wide world of horticulture. Also, where the pond is concerned, they are probably the most important.

Oxygenators

Oxygenators are invariably green; they rarely flower and seem to spend their lives suspended in the water, growing rapidly and never when you want them to. During the daytime they convert dissolved carbon dioxide, given off by the fish, into oxygen. They also consume minerals and nutrients that otherwise would be used by opportunist and troublesome algae. A good selection of oxygenating plants will also provide effective cover for all manner of water creatures, protecting fish against marauding herons, and providing spawning grounds for fish, as well as amphibious and insectivorous wildlife.

Most garden centres will offer oxygenating plants, from outside tanks, usually sold as small bunches of stems linked by a heavy metal weight. You simply drop these bunches into the pond – you don't need planting baskets or compost. The weights will take the bases of the bunches down, and they will find their own level (depending on the amount of leaves) and start to grow.

	site	Ponds which receive direct sunlight for at least part of the day
	temp	All are moderately hardy, tolerating temperatures down to -10°C (-14°F)
	general care	Most grow by simply being placed into the pond. They usually do not need special care
	thinning	Thinning should take place three times during the growing season
	pests & diseases	Relatively trouble free. Oxygenators are not normally troubled by pests and diseases

Overcrowding

Most oxygenators will grow rapidly, especially in warm summers, and can cause the pond to become congested. You should, therefore, hook out a bucketful or two of excess 'weed', and perhaps do this two or three times during the summer. Cut off surplus growth if accessible or use a garden rake to pull out excessive growth. This will, curiously, make the weed grow faster, and in turn make it more efficient at filtering and conditioning the water.

Carefully check through the foliage as you remove it, spread it out by the side of the pond and leave it for a day so that any creatures caught up in it can crawl back into the water.

After this, add the semi-dried weed to the compost heap. On no account take it to your local pond or stream to keep it alive. Many misguided aquarists and pond owners have done this in the past, and have introduced plants that have quickly crowded out our native pond plant species, upsetting the ecology of our natural waterways.

Oxygenator selection

It is a good idea to select several different species of oxygenator so that different types of wildlife will be attracted. All wild pond-inhabiting creatures have their particular likes and dislikes, and a variety of foliage shapes and growth habits will offer the most habitats.

Callitriche

This is known as the autumn starwort (*Callitriche hermaphroditica*). It is a delicate plant with vivid green foliage and fragile stems, growing rapidly from single crowns. Unfortunately, it is not easy to distinguish between this species and other forms of Callitriche, as the shape of the leaves and the overall habit of the plant can vary enormously as a result of ambient conditions. This plant grows all year round and is a good choice for ponds that receive all-day sun. It prefers water down to a depth of 45cm (18in). Small white flowers appear throughout summer, but these are hardly noticeable. It works as well in moving water as it does in still pools. Like all submerged oxygenators, it will need attention so that it does not become invasive. It is, however, prone to damage by heavy-finned fish.

Ceratophyllum

Hornwort (*Ceratophyllum demersum*) is a free-floating plant with dark green, feathery foliage. It looks a little like an underwater conifer tree, growing in a mat just underneath the surface of the water. It does not have roots, so there is no need to pot it or plant it in the soil at the bottom of the pond – simply place it in the pond. Where the stems come into contact with the sides of the pond, or underground stones or the mud at the bottom, modified leaves are produced which help to anchor the plants. This many-branched oxygenator will grow well in sunny or partially shaded ponds. If you want to keep it in one location, secure it with a large stone and a rubber band. It makes a good spawning ground for fish in spring and is somewhat resistant to the ravages of koi.

Eleocharis

Hairgrass plants (forms of Eleocharis) are usually regarded as submerged plants for aquaria rather than outdoor ponds; the hardier forms can also be grown as bog garden plants. One that is appropriate as an outdoor oxygenator is *Eleocharis acicularis*. It is a little different to most other oxygenators in that it covers the soil at the bottom of the pond or the soil in a planting basket with dense tufts of grass-like leaves. Because the mat of foliage hugs the soil in this way, it gives the impression of an underwater lawn. In reality, the delicate beauty of the leaves tends to be lost among the other, more vigorous and broader-leaved oxygenators. Minuscule flowers appear in summer. Propagation is easy – during the growing season break away clumps and replant.

Elodea

Canadian pond weed (*Elodea canadensis*) is probably the most commonly seen oxygenator; it is hardy, vigorous and ideal for new ponds. Lance-shaped dark green leaves are held on long stems. It is one of the most efficient of all oxygenating plants, but it can also be very invasive. Because of this, some authorities maintain that it should not be grown, particularly if you have a large pond that makes thinning difficult. However, it is worth trying if you have a small pond where other oxygenators have failed to establish. If it is confined to a planting basket, it can be easily controlled. Canadian pond weed can also be used in contained water features, such as a tub, barrel or glazed pot, where it can be regularly trimmed to maintain its spread. It prefers water that is alkaline and grows best when planted in soil containing a high proportion of fine sand. Propagate it from stem cuttings in spring or summer. It is a favourite food of goldfish and koi, and some reports say that it secretes a chemical compound that reduces populations of mosquito larvae.

Myriophyllum

Myriophyllum is commonly known as milfoil. There are about 40 different water milfoils worldwide, all making superb perennial oxygenating plants with attractive blue green or brown fern-like leaves in artistic whorls. Milfoils are loved by fish as a spawning ground and provide an excellent refuge for young fish, in addition to oxygenating the pond.

The most common milfoil found in domestic outdoor ponds is *Myriophyllum aquaticum*. This oxygenator has very dense, ferny foliage that emerges stiffly from the water, often as high as 30cm (12in). It is a tropical species, preferring a pond that is situated in the full sun. Due to its slightly tender nature, *Myriophyllum aquaticum* is just as suitable for indoor tropical aquaria.

Outdoors, grow Myriophyllum in baskets of loamy soil, at a depth of 1m (3ft) for *M. aquaticum*. The plant tends to die back in winter to dormant crowns that rest well beneath the surface of the water, or it is liable to become damaged by frosts. These crowns then re-emerge below the surface in spring. It is recommended for use in small ponds because it is not particularly invasive. Self-rooting stems are often produced, and these may be separated and replanted. Otherwise, take stem cuttings in spring or summer to propagate. Young growth can often get eaten by fish.

Potamogeton

Curled pond weed (*Potamogeton crispus*) produces long, wavy green or bronze leaves. However, both the stems and the leaves of this plant are somewhat brittle. It can be a slow plant to establish but it is extremely sturdy, making the plant particularly good for ponds with waterfalls or fountains. Once established, however, it can quickly spread, so it will need regular thinning throughout the growing season. The branched rhizomes spread rapidly in the mud at the bottom of ponds. It grows to a depth of about 1m (3ft). It more closely resembles seaweed than a flowering plant, with its translucent, crisp and crimped foliage. Although it does produce tiny crimson and yellow flower spikes just above the surface of the water in the summer, these are fairly insignificant and it is not worth selecting the plant on this criterion. *Potamogeton crispus* is a tough plant, with a good degree of resistance to frost and ice, but does prefer a pond situated in the full sun. *P. crispus* tolerates polluted water better than most of the oxygenators. It makes a good spawning ground for fish, and is an important source of food for waterfowl. Take cuttings at any stage during the growth period. Fasten them together in bunches with thin strips and plant them in their permanent positions.

Floating Water Plants

Floating water plants do not require potting and they are not particular as to the condition of the soil beneath them. Some do produce a few straggly roots that simply dangle in the water, but because they just float, the depth of the water is not important. These plants are, it has to be said, the ultimate in easy gardening.

There are two main types of floating water plant: the carpeters (such as Lemna and Azolla), which produce tiny leaves that can cover the entire pond if left unchecked, and the non-carpeters (such as Eichhornia and Pistia), which have larger leaves and are generally less invasive.

Most will oxygenate the water in a small way. The principle reason for growing them, however, is their facility of shading fish and amphibious creatures from the sun, while at the same time protecting them from predators. An often forgotten benefit of floating plants is that the shade they afford the water can also significantly reduce the incidence of algae, both the filamentous types (such as blanketweed) and the free-floating types.

Too many floating plants in a pond, of course, can reduce the amount of available oxygen, which harms fish, so do not let these floaters completely cover the pond's surface. Some plants will increase their size and number rapidly, and so regular thinning out is required.

These plants are the easiest of any aquatics to plant, as you just drop them into the pond (unlike with submerged oxygenators, you do not even need to weigh them down). They tend to die down during late autumn, to survive the winter as dormant buds or seeds, resting in the mud at the bottom of the pond. In spring, when the weather warms, they burst into life again.

Azolla filiculoides

Fairy moss

This is neither a moss, nor a flowering plant, but a charming tiny fern that collects into dense masses. The derivation of its botanical name should come as no surprise: from the Greek *azo*, to dry up, and *ollymi*, to kill, ie. the plant that is killed by drought!

Pale blue-green, lacy deciduous fronds, 1cm (⅖in) across, turn rich reddish purple during autumn. The simple, short and slender roots absorb nourishment from the pond water. Position Azolla in full sun or light shade. In spring, drop a few fronds directly onto the water, but not in moving water. It is a prolific spreader, so do not introduce into large, inaccessible ponds as it will rapidly become out of hand. Net out unwanted plants during the growing season. Plants survive winter as submerged dormant buds, but as frost injury is possible overwinter some plantlets under glass in a jar of water and soil. Propagate by removing a few fronds during mid-spring and introduce them to a new pond.

Azolla filiculoides

site	Both plants grow best in a pond that is in full sun or partial shade	
temp	*A. filiculoides*: barely hardy, down to -5°C (23°F). *E. crassipes*: tender, 5°C (40°F)	
general care	For both *A. filiculoides* and *E. crassipes*, drop the new plants into the pond during spring	
thinning	*A. filiculoides*: net unwanted plants any time. *E. crassipes*: hand pick in summer/autumn	
pests & diseases	Both plants are relatively trouble free. Pests and diseases do not usually cause them any problems	

Eichhornia crassipes

Water hyacinth

This is a robust, free-floating plant and a prolific spreader in hot climates. Bluish-violet blooms, not unlike small hyacinths, rise above the water surface from mid-summer to early autumn. They perform best in full sun.

Eichhornia crassipes

Remove water hyacinths from the pond during mid-autumn. Divide and store them in wet mud or moist pots in a greenhouse or coldframe until the spring. They can be re-sited in the pond from mid-spring onwards, but it is worth hardening them off gradually; the plant tissue will have become tender, and could be damaged if there is a severe late frost. Separating the clumps in spring, or in the autumn as they are removed to their winter quarters, is the best way to propagate water hyacinths.

Some countries use water hyacinths as a form of biological filtration in water treatment sites in order to treat sewage.

	SPRING	SUMMER	AUTUMN	WINTER	height (cm)	spread (cm)	flower colour	
Azolla filiculoides	🌱🌱🌱	🌱🌱🌱			2.5	100+		Do not use in large ponds
Eichhornia crassipes		🌱🌱 ✹✹	✹		30	100		Also good in tropical aquaria

 planting　✹ flowering

Hottonia
Water violet

If you want to grow a floating water plant with attractive flowers held well above the surface of the water, and which doubles as an oxygenator, then you can hardly do better than to choose the water violet. It is a beautiful, hardy herbaceous perennial that is not a violet at all, but a member of the primula family.

Spikes of white or pale lilac flowers 23–25cm (9–10in) high, appear from early to mid-summer. The mid-green feathery leaves, which float just below the surface of the water, are efficient oxygenators, while other less divided leaves are also under the water but do not oxygenate. The flowers, when combined with leaves that protrude out of the water, give this plant the appearance of a marginal.

Hottonia grows best when positioned in the full sun or medium shade. Individual plants are placed into the water during spring. In shallow water they will root in the mud at the bottom, but in deeper water they will rest just below the surface – at least for the early part of the summer – before they throw up the flower spikes.

Thin out excessive growth during the summer. In autumn, plants die down and

site	Grows best in a pond that is in full sun or medium shade
temp	Very hardy, tolerating temperatures down to -20°C (-4°F)
general care	When first growing these plants, drop them into the pond during the spring
thinning	Rake out excessive growth in summer; can spread up to 1m² (1yd²)
pests & diseases	These plants are relatively trouble free. Pests and diseases do not usually cause them any problems

pass the winter as dormant buds (known as turions). These will sink to the bottom of the pond, rising again and producing new growth in spring.

Still as opposed to moving water is preferred, so it is best to avoid planting the water violet in ponds that are fed by cascades or which contain fountains. As well as being suitable for a small garden pond, they are excellent for a larger wildlife pond.

Propagate by dividing larger plants during summer or else by rooting stem cuttings in wet mud. Gather any submerged seeds in the autumn and grow them on in trays of mud.

Hottonia inflata – referred to as the featherfoil – is similar to but smaller than *H. palustris*, with white flowers. However, it is a rare species and therefore may be difficult to find.

Hottonia palustris

	SPRING	SUMMER	AUTUMN	WINTER	height (cm)	spread (cm)	flower colour	
Hottonia inflata	🌱🌱🌱	✹✹			30	100	⬜	Avoid moving water
H. palustris	🌱🌱🌱	✹✹			37	100	⬜	Good for oxygenating the water

planting ✹ flowering

Hydrocharis morsus-ranae
Frogbit

The flowers of the frogbit, a rather beautiful floater, look as if they are trilliums – woodland dwelling plants with only three petals. In its native countries of northern Europe it can, if not kept in check, quickly overcrowd and block up small pools and waterways. Frogbit is always best grown in a still pond, with water that is neutral to alkaline. Normally, only this species is available.

This attractive floating plant looks very similar to a tiny waterlily. From mid- to late summer, rising elegantly above the surface of the water, white three-petalled, papery flowers appear, each with a yellow centre. The leaves are small, deciduous, rounded or heart-shaped, and are green-bronze in colour. The leaves are both floating and raised above the water surface.

When starting these plants off in your pond, drop young frogbits in the water during spring. The best light conditions for these plants are full sun to very light shade. They will perform at their best in a still pond. Thin out established plants several times a year using a net to limit the spread.

Hydrocharis morsus-ranae is useful as a surface cover plant for wildlife ponds. It tolerates temperatures as low as -20°C (-4°F) and survives the winter as dormant buds, which fall to the bottom of the pond. However, the water must not be allowed to freeze at the bottom of the pond, because this is where the buds are protected from the severe cold, as the overwintering buds hibernate.

Hydrocharis morsus-ranae

	site	Grows best in a pond that is in full sun or light shade
	temp	Very hardy, tolerating temperatures down to -20°C (-4°F)
	general care	When first growing these plants, drop them into the pond during the spring
	thinning	Net out unwanted plants at any time of the year; can spread up to 1m² (1yd²)
	pests & diseases	Water snails have a liking for the leaves but no major problems apart from this

Hydrocharis morsus-ranae

Propagate by carefully removing young plantlets that form on runners (rather like strawberries, but on a much smaller scale). This can be done at any time during the growing season.

Watch out for attack from water snails, which nibble at the leaves.

Lemna minor
Duckweed

If you introduce duckweed to your pond, either accidentally or on purpose, the pond will soon be covered with a pale, lime-green carpet. Its common name probably comes from the fact that ducks on larger ponds do tend to nuzzle around in it for food.

The form that is generally found in garden ponds is *Lemna minor*. The leaves are minute, almost translucent, deciduous and in various shapes, but mostly oval. Thousands of them abut each other to form the familiar covering over the surface of the water. Each individual leaf usually produces a single, dangling root. The tiny summer flowers are insignificant.

To plant, simply drop several leaves with roots into the pond, generally in spring. It grows best in still, or nearly still water, and in either full sun or light shade.

A couple of individual leaves can increase and cover up to 1m² (1yd²) in a year, but thereafter rapid covering of ponds can take place. Thin it out occasionally to prevent it from covering and choking the whole pond.

Propagation takes the form of simply

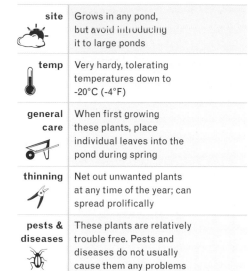

site	Grows in any pond, but avoid introducing it to large ponds
temp	Very hardy, tolerating temperatures down to -20°C (-4°F)
general care	When first growing these plants, place individual leaves into the pond during spring
thinning	Net out unwanted plants at any time of the year; can spread prolifically
pests & diseases	These plants are relatively trouble free. Pests and diseases do not usually cause them any problems

redistributing some of the leaves to a different pond. Duckweed survives in winter as dormant buds on the bottom of the pond.

The ivy-leaved duckweed (*L. trisulca*) is somewhat less invasive than the common kind and produces a mass of star-shaped leaves, frequently floating just beneath the surface. *L. gibba*, often referred to as the thick or gibbous duckweed, has rounded, swollen leaves and is particularly invasive. *L. polyrhiza* (also known as *Spirodela polyrhiza* and commonly referred to as great duckweed) has larger, rounder leaves than the normal kinds, and each has a small 'tuft' of roots attached. It is very invasive.

Most experts are asked how to get rid off duckweed, rather than how to grow it. If you do not want it, check carefully each new water plant for the presence of duckweed before it is introduced to the pond.

Lemna minor

	SPRING	SUMMER	AUTUMN	WINTER	height (cm)	spread (cm)	flower colour	
Lemna gibba	🌱🌱🌱	●●●			100+			Rounded, swollen leaves
L. minor	🌱🌱🌱	●●●			100+			Grows best in a still pond
L. polyrhiza	🌱🌱🌱	●●●			100+			The most invasive species
L. trisulca	🌱🌱🌱	●●●			100+			Star-shaped leaves

🌱 planting ● flowering

Stratiotes aloides

Water soldier
or Water aloe

This intriguing plant is often described as resembling a floating pineapple top. It is a semi-evergreen perennial, free-floating, and held partly below and partly above the water. Curiously, plants sink and multiply after flowering, and rise again some weeks later, when surplus offsets can be thinned with a net. Normally just the single species, *Stratiotes aloides*, is available. It is a good choice for wildlife ponds.

Separate male and female flowers are formed from early to late summer. Females are small, creamy white and papery, tucked in the leaf axils. The male flowers are produced in clusters in a pinkish spathe.

The leaves are dark olive green, narrow and stiff-toothed, arranged in neat, stalkless rosettes.

Water soldiers perform best when positioned in a pond that is in the full sun. They usually overwinter at the bottom of the pond. Stratiotes can be prolific and needs to be kept in check, but because the individual plants are so large, they can be removed by hand if necessary.

New plants form as small water buds on spreading stems: separating the clumps in spring and summer is the best way to propagate them.

It is a fully hardy plant, tolerating temperatures down as low as -15°C (5°F). It is relatively trouble free from pests and diseases.

Found naturally in still or slow-moving water throughout Europe, these plants prefer alkaline or limestone waters, which is why they do not always transfer successfully from one pond to another.

site	Grows best in full sun or light shade, and with alkaline or limestone waters
temp	Hardy, tolerating temperatures down to -15°C (5°F)
general care	When first growing these plants, place them into the pond during spring
thinning	Hand pick unwanted plants at any time of the year as it can spread
pests & diseases	These plants are relatively trouble free. Pests and diseases do not usually cause them any problems

Stratiotes aloides

Trapa natans
Water chestnut

Trapa natans is the familiar water chestnut used in Chinese cuisine. The edible fruits are large and thorny, but do not be tempted to nibble any that may be growing in your pond as they are poisonous when raw. Normally this is the only species available.

This is an aquatic plant with roots but the leaves appear to be floating independently. It is unlike any other pond plant, with rosettes of deciduous, angular, toothed leaves, each carried on an inflated stalk. The flowers appear in summer; they are small, white and well hidden among the leaves.

Because Trapa throws down hair-like roots into the mud, the water depth is important. Grow it in a depth of 30–45cm (12–18in) for best results. Although its dormant fruits will survive winters in the bottom of the pond, germination may be erratic in cold climates. Warm summers help increase germination. To plant, just drop young plants into the water in spring. Propagate by sowing the spiny fruits in the pool mud in spring; they will give rise to a stem from which floating leaves develop.

Trapa natans

	site	Both prefer a still pond in full sun or light shade, in slightly acidic water
	temp	*T. natans*: barely hardy, down to -5°C (23°F). *U. vulgaris*: hardy, down to -20°C (-4°F)
	general care	When first growing these plants, place both species into the pond during spring
	thinning	For both species, scoop out unwanted plants at any time of the year
	pests & diseases	Both plants are relatively trouble free. Pests and diseases do not usually cause them any problems

Utricularia vulgaris
Bladderwort

This is an unusual floating plant in that it is a meat-eater! It traps minute aquatic creatures in its mass of fine foliage and consumes them.

The plant resembles pieces of floating hair-net and can be mistaken for some types of 'string' algae. However, the benefits of growing bladderwort are that it affords good shelter and food for fish, and in summer it produces attractive, small, deep orange snapdragon-like flowers rising above the water's surface. As there are no roots, neither soil nor potting is necessary. Several species of Utricularia are available from specialist suppliers, but make sure that plants you buy are hardy and not for use in aquaria.

Utricularia vulgaris (and Nymphaea)

	SPRING	SUMMER	AUTUMN	WINTER	height (cm)	spread (cm)	flower colour	
Trapa natans	🌱 🌱 🌱	● ● ●			100		☐	Edible water chestnuts when cooked
Utricularia vulgaris	🌱 🌱	● ● ●			50		■	Carnivorous plant

🌱 planting   ✺ flowering

Flowering Water Plants

There is a clear distinction between flowering water plants and marginals (featured later in the book). The former are plants growing within the pond, anchored in mud or planting containers, but which have leaves and flowers on top of the water or rising above it. Marginals grow at the very edge of the water, regardless of whether their roots are growing in underwater mud or merely in damp soil.

As far as flowering water plants are concerned, the classic example is the waterlily. It outstrips all other pond plants by its popularity and the sheer number of species and cultivars available. Waterlilies also typify one of the most important aspects of the category, in that the vigour of their surface spread and the depth of water to which they are most suited means that forms must be chosen carefully and wisely. Depending on the variety, the recommended planting depth for waterlilies can be anywhere from 10–90cm (4–36in), although most thrive in the depth range of 25–45cm (10–18in).

Most flowering water plants help to keep the pond water clear by absorbing certain chemical compounds via their roots. They also provide a degree of oxygenation, albeit tiny, and afford shelter and food for fish. But the overriding benefits are that they are attractive to look at. Often the flowers on these plants are like nothing else in the garden, such as the lotus (Nelumbo) and pond lilies (Nuphar), which make them a good talking point.

There are flowering aquatics for ponds in full sun, some for partial shade, some for very deep water and some for water that is constantly splashing through the actions of waterfalls or fountains.

Keeping plants in containers, rather than allowing them the free run of the mud in the bottom of the pond, makes them easy to control and, generally, does not restrict their growth adversely or reduce their ability to flower.

Aponogeton distachyos

Water hawthorn *or* Cape pondweed

The water hawthorn is an excellent plant for deep-water ponds. It has attractive floating leaves that are more or less evergreen; and the vanilla-like fragrance of the blooms is powerful and lingering. After the main spring crop of blooms, plants generally collapse until late summer, when they often disappear from sight altogether, unless growing in the shade.

By mid-autumn, however, they have usually produced a fresh set of leaves and start flowering again, sometimes through to early winter in mild parts. Aponogeton is a native of the southern tip of the African continent, and has not acclimatized to the more temperate flowering seasons of most of Europe and America, which is perhaps why it produces two flushes of flowers every year.

The flowers are comprised of white with waxy petals and jet-black anthers, in forked spikes that almost float on the surface of the water. The leaves are oval, long, and mid-green with brown blotches, floating on the surface of the water. The plant is evergreen in mild parts. You do not need a full-sized pond in order to grow Aponogeton: even a water barrel could sustain a plant or two.

Set out water hawthorns in spring, by planting the tubers – or young plants – 45cm (18in) apart, in small isolated groups in baskets, or directly into soil. They perform well in full sun, but with light shade they have a longer flowering period. Remove dead foliage as it appears.

The freely produced green seeds can be found floating on the surface of the pond during late summer and autumn. To propagate the water hawthorn, net out some of the ripe seeds, and sow them straight away in containers of wet, loamy compost indoors. Seeds must be sown immediately and not be allowed to dry out. Alternatively, divide mature, established plants in late spring. They can grow to 10cm (4in) above the water and spread to around 60cm (24in).

site	Performs well in full sun, but flowers for longer when in light shade
temp	Hardy, tolerating temperatures to -5°C (23°F), or colder in deeper water
general care	When first growing aponogetons, plant them in baskets or directly into the soil during spring
thinning	Lift and discard unwanted plants any time, or divide overcrowded plants in spring
pests & diseases	Snails can be especially destructive to the leaves, particularly of young aponogeton plants

Aponogeton distachyos

Hippuris vulgaris

Mare's tail

Most gardening experts have been asked at some time in their careers how to eradicate one of the worst and rampant weeds of all – horsetail (*Equisetum vulgare*). Fortunately, although there is a similarity in habit, the plant recommended here bears no relation to that weed.

The name does sound slightly similar, however, and there is at least one good equisetum that is sometimes grown as a marginal, which only adds to the confusion between horsetail and mare's tail.

Hippuris vulgaris – normally only this species is available – is an attractive perennial, found growing naturally in waterways throughout mainland Europe where its strongly spreading rhizome forms large colonies.

Although tiny, insignificant green flowers appear during summer, the strength of the plants comes with its foliage. Numerous short, narrow, deciduous needle-like leaves come in spirals up the stalks. The underwater portions of the stems tend to carry thinner and more flimsy leaves.

Plants extend their leafy stems up to 23–37.5cm (9–15in) above the water surface, depending on the depth of water in which they are growing. Hippuris does have a preferred depth of around 60cm (24in),

site	Full sun, but it is also a good choice for a shady pond where little else will grow
temp	Very hardy, tolerating temperatures only down to -20°C (-4°F)
general care	Set young plants or rhizomes into planting baskets during spring. Remove dead foliage in autumn
thinning	Lift out unwanted plants any time, or divide overcrowded plants in spring
pests & diseases	These plants are relatively trouble free. Pests and diseases do not usually cause them any problems

but will grow adequately in depths considerably less or more. It spreads to around 45cm (18in).

The recommended method of propagation for the amateur is by division, and this should be carried out at any time during spring.

Hippuris vulgaris

Iris fulva

This is a pale copper-red iris, a fairly unusual colour for a water iris. Its natural habitats are the warm, wetlands of south Louisiana in the USA, hence it is classified by specialists to be in a small group called the Louisiana Irises (see also _Iris_ x _fulvala_).

All water irises have many forms of flowers: single flowers have three petals and three upright standards (almost petals). The petals have what is known as a signal flash in the centre near the stem, and this can be of a variety of colours. Double flowers have six petals, where the standards have actually become petals.

There are many Louisiana hybrids still being bred, particularly in North America, and these are something to look forward to. They have so far produced some stunning results, with flowers of pale pink, white, red, yellow, blue and purple, some with ruffled edges and others so double that they look more like a camellia than an iris.

Iris fulva 'Dwarf Terracotta'

Iris fulva 'Marvell Gold'

site	_Iris fulva_ grows best planted in a still pond which is in the full sun
temp	Frost hardy, tolerating temperatures only down to -5°C (23°F)
general care	Grow these plants in containers as they can spread indefinitely and take over the pond
thinning	Divide plants every third year. Pot up the offshoots with garden soil
pests & diseases	Aphids, iris sawfly, caterpillars and earwigs can cause problems to these plants

Iris fulva produces lush green foliage, appearing early in the spring, giving the pond a luxuriant, green effect before much of the other garden foliage has emerged.

Plant between mid-spring and mid-summer. Remove dead leaves and deadhead the faded flowers before seeds are set (unless you are collecting seed), otherwise flowering may be reduced the following year.

	SPRING	SUMMER	AUTUMN	WINTER	height (cm)	spread (cm)	flower colour	
Iris fulva 'Dwarf Terracotta'					45–80	100+		Rare colour for a water iris
I. fulva 'Marvell Gold'					45–80	100+		Worth searching for

🌱 planting   ✹ flowering

Iris laevigata

Japanese water iris *or* Rabbit ear iris

Iris laevigata is arguably the most important iris for growing in water. It originated in Japan, hence its common name, and has been used throughout the centuries in Oriental literature and iconography. The West has accepted this particular iris as a symbol of elegance and peace.

The three-petalled blooms of straight *Iris laevigata* are about 12.5cm (5in) across, and are borne on 60cm (2ft) high stems. The first flowers open in early summer, and are a clear blue-violet with a yellow line down the centre of each petal. If plants are enjoying life in the right conditions, a second flush of flowers may appear in late summer or early autumn.

There are many varieties of *I. laevigata*, but among the best is 'Alba', with its pure white, single blooms; 'Snowdrift', on the other hand, has double flowers; 'Mottled Beauty' has white flowers with pale mauve mottling at the base, while 'Elegante' has white flowers with heavy dark blue edging. One of the most popular cultivars, with similar white and dark blue markings, is the

Iris laevigata

site	Grows best in a still pond which is in full sun or light shade
temp	Hardy, tolerating temperatures down to -5°C (23°F)
general care	Grow these plants in containers during spring as they can spread indefinitely and take over the pond
thinning	Divide plants every three or four years. Pot up the offshoots with garden soil
pests & diseases	Aphids, iris sawfly, caterpillars and earwigs can cause problems to these plants

double flowered 'Colchesterensis' (sometimes seen as 'Colchesteri'). 'Variegata' has a pale blue single flower with a green and white variegated flag.

	SPRING	SUMMER	AUTUMN	WINTER	height (cm)	spread (cm)	flower colour	
Iris laevigata	🌱🌱🌱	✹ ✹ ✹			60-90	100+	▨	Second flush of flowers possible
I. laevigata 'Alba'	🌱🌱🌱	✹ ✹ ✹			60-90	100+	☐	Single flowers
I. laevigata 'Colchesterensis'	🌱🌱🌱	✹ ✹ ✹			60-90	100+	☐	Double flowers
I. laevigata 'Elegante'	🌱🌱🌱	✹ ✹ ✹			60-90	100+	☐	Single flowers
I. laevigata 'Mottled Beauty'	🌱🌱🌱	✹ ✹ ✹			60-90	100+	▨	Single flowers
I. laevigata 'Snowdrift'	🌱🌱🌱	✹ ✹ ✹			60-90	100+	☐	Double flowers
I. laevigata 'Variegata'	🌱🌱🌱	✹ ✹ ✹			60-90	100+	▨	Green and white variegated flag
I. laevigata 'Weymouth Midnight'	🌱🌱🌱	✹ ✹			60-90	100+	▓	Double flowers

 planting   ✹ *flowering*

Iris pseudacorus

Yellow flag iris

The yellow flag iris is the most common of water irises, and roots of it will grow vigorously. It will, within reason, grow in any depth of water. This iris can be extremely prolific, spreading rapidly across the pond.

It is possible to roughly chop up small sections with leaves and weigh them down in 37cm (15in) of water, and for the plant to grow away with great success. If you have a smallish pond, it would be sensible to divide your clump every couple of years for the best results.

Regardless of its vigour, it is certainly worth a place in the water garden. The species produces large golden flowers and brown signal flashes, it needs a lot of room in which to grow, so should only be planted into a medium to large pond. There are a

	site	Grows best in a pond which is in full sun or light shade
	temp	Very hardy, tolerating temperatures down to -20°C (-4°F)
	general care	Grow these plants in containers during spring as they can spread indefinitely and take over the pond
	thinning	Divide plants every third year. Pot up the offshoots with garden soil
	pests & diseases	Iris sawfly and caterpillars are the only pests that can cause these plants a problem

Iris pseudacorus

number of excellent varieties. One of the most popular is 'Flore Pleno': this is a hose-in-hose iris, which means that the flower is constructed from many blooms, each one growing inside another.

More diminutive are 'Golden Queen', a completely golden iris with no brown signal flashes, and *Iris pseudacorus* var *bastardii*, a cream variety with pale brown signals. For something completely different you could always try 'Ecru', an almost white flower with dark brown signals. 'Alba' is a pale creamy white form with brown signals, and 'Roy Davidson' has golden yellow flowers, heavily veined with brown down the whole of the petal, making the flower look extremely dark and inviting.

'Variegata' has golden flowers with deep yellow and green variegated leaves. The actual variegation is not stable, meaning

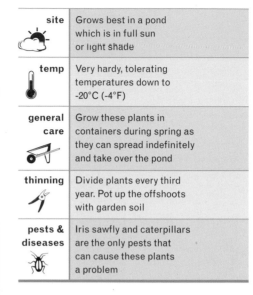

Iris pseudacorus

that the flag reverts to green in late summer, but in the following spring it will once again emerge with wonderful bright yellow and green colourings.

Finally, there is a vigorous cultivar with the unlikely name of 'Turnipseed'. The flag is extremely strong, able to reach a height of 2m (6ft), with golden yellow flowers.

	SPRING	SUMMER	AUTUMN	WINTER	height (cm)	spread (cm)	flower colour	
Iris pseudacorus	planting planting planting flowering	flowering			200	100+		Most common water iris
I. pseudacorus 'Alba'	planting planting planting flowering	flowering			200	100+		Long green leaves
I. pseudacorus var bastardii	planting planting planting flowering	flowering			150	100+		A more diminutive plant
I. pseudacorus 'Ecru'	planting planting planting flowering	flowering			200	100+		An unusual iris
I. pseudacorus 'Flore Pleno'	planting planting planting flowering	flowering			200	100+		Hose-in-hose iris
I. pseudacorus 'Golden Queen'	planting planting planting flowering	flowering			150	100+		One of the smaller cultivars
I. pseudacorus 'Roy Davidson'	planting planting planting flowering	flowering			200	100+		Heavily veined flowers
I. pseudacorus 'Turnipseed'	planting planting planting	flowering			200	100+		One of the tallest cultivars
I. pseudacorus 'Variegata'	planting planting planting flowering	flowering			200	100+		Yellow and green variegated leaves

Iris versicolor

American blue flag

Although this plant is referred to as the American blue flag, it actually has a bright green flag (the green leaf part of the plant) with a profusion of small flowers. Its flower stalks are 45–60cm (18–24in) high, the leaves reaching a little higher still.

It can come in various colours, the norm being pale blue, through to darker blue, but there are white forms as well as many named varieties. One of these varieties is

Iris versicolor

'Kermesina', a deep wine red with golden signals. 'Mysterious Monique' has deep red flowers that almost verge to purple. There are also a number of heavily veined varieties, including 'Between the Lines', a pure white with pale blue veining.

site	Grows best in a still pond which is in full sun or light shade
temp	Hardy, tolerating temperatures down to -15°C (5°F)
general care	Grow these plants in containers during spring as they can spread indefinitely and take over the pond
thinning	Divide plants every three or four years. Pot up the offshoots with garden soil
pests & diseases	Aphids, iris sawfly, caterpillars and snails can cause problems to these plants

	SPRING	SUMMER	AUTUMN	WINTER	height (cm)	spread (cm)	flower colour	
Iris versicolor	planting planting planting	flowering flowering flowering			45-60	100+		Many small flowers
I. versicolor 'Between the Lines'	planting planting planting	flowering flowering flowering			45-60	100+		Veining is a feature of the flowers
I. versicolor 'Kermesina'	planting planting planting	flowering flowering flowering			45-60	100+		The most popular cultivar
I. versicolor 'Mysterious Monique'	planting planting planting	flowering flowering flowering			45-60	100+		One of the darkest flowered forms

  planting flowering

Iris x fulvala

As with *Iris fulva*, this is one of the Louisiana irises, which are naturally distributed in the warm and wetlands of the southern USA. In appearance, however, this iris is totally different. It is a much showier iris, with large, rich red-purple flowers and golden signals.

Similar characteristics are that it produces lush green foliage early in the spring, before many other types of garden plants have come in to leaf. It is a robust, rhizomatous iris.

Iris x *fulvala* plants prefer a pond or waterway in full sun, but they will generally perform well in light shade.

Newly bought containerized plants will be growing in a suitable soil, but if you are replanting, use good, clean garden soil from a part of the garden that has not recently been dressed with fertilizer. Remove twigs, weeds, old leaves or anything likely to decay and foul the water.

Plant between mid-spring and mid-summer. Little general care is required once plants are established. Remove any dead or scrappy leaves when seen. Deadhead the faded flowers before seeds are set (unless you are wanting to collect the seed), otherwise flowering may be reduced the following year.

site	Grows best in a still pond which is in full sun or light shade
temp	Hardy, tolerating temperatures only down to -15°C (5°F)
general care	When first growing these plants, site them in the pond, or bog garden, during the spring
thinning	Grow pond plants in containers to prevent spreading
pests & diseases	Aphids, iris sawfly, caterpillars and earwigs can cause problems to these plants

This iris will benefit from lifting and dividing every three or four years during mid- to late spring. Use garden soil to pot up the offshoots into new aquatic pots. To prevent fish from disturbing the soil, and small soil particles floating away, place gravel or small stones over the surface.

Aphids, caterpillars and earwigs, are the main pests, while there are several viruses that can affect flowering and leaf production. Because of the risk of chemical run-off in to the pondwater, insecticide controls are not possible, so the pests should simply be washed off with a jet of water from a hosepipe, and allowed to sink or swim! However, none of these problems is generally considered to be life-threatening.

This iris will grow equally well in a bog garden or pond.

Iris x fulvala

	SPRING	SUMMER	AUTUMN	WINTER	height (cm)	spread (cm)	flower colour	
Iris x *fulvala*	🌱🌱🌱	☀️ ☀️			45	100+		Will thrive in a bog garden
I. x *fulvala* 'Violacea'	🌱🌱🌱	☀️ ☀️			45	100+		Deep violet colour

🌱 planting　☀️ flowering

Nelumbo
Lotus blossom

Even if you live in a cooler climate, as long as you have a pond you can grow lotuses. However, unless you live in areas where these plants grow well outdoors all year round, either in gardens or naturally in waterways, you will have to search for them from specialist dealers. The plants will reward you, as long as you also expend a little effort in accommodating their idiosyncracies.

There are two species, the hardiest of which is the north American chinkapin (*Nelumbo lutea*). It is the smaller of the two, growing to 2m (6ft) in height, with large and showy yellow blossoms. Although not often grown outside in more cooler regions, it is a reasonably hardy plant and should produce plenty of typical plate-like foliage, if not many flowers.

The Asian sacred lotus (*N. nucifera*) is a giant of a plant in its original form, but one which has given us a range of dwarf cultivars. Try the white, pink-edged 'Chawan Basu' or the carmine-pink 'Pekinensis Rubra'. Instead of growing them in the pool try them in a large tub or container at the waterside. When container grown, they can be easily moved indoors during the autumn for overwintering in a frost-free place.

Most lotuses open their flowers early in the day – often before dawn – and will produce a second flush of flowers during late summer or even early autumn, as long as there has been a fairly hot summer.

Nelumbo nucifera

Nelumbo nucifera

site		Grows best in full sun, in warm water that often exceeds 15°C (60°F)
temp		Not hardy, tolerating temperatures only down to 1°C (34°F)
general care		Overwinter in containers in a frost-free place. Only place outdoors once risk of frosts have passed
thinning		Keep potted in containers as they can spread; divide every second year
pests & diseases		Aphids can cause a few problems but apart from this, these plants are relatively trouble free

	SPRING	SUMMER	AUTUMN	WINTER	height (cm)	spread (cm)	flower colour	
Nelumbo 'Ben Gibson'	🌱🌱🌱	● ●	●		120	100	▨	Fully double
N. 'Chawan Basu'	🌱🌱🌱	● ●	●		120	100	☐	A dwarf hybrid
N. lutea	🌱🌱🌱	● ●	●		200	100	▨	The hardiest form
N. nucifera	🌱🌱🌱	● ●	●		250	100	☐	Lasts well as cut flowers
N. 'Pekinensis Rubra'	🌱🌱🌱	● ●	●		120	100	▨	A dwarf hybrid

🌱 *planting*   ● *flowering*

Nuphar

Yellow pond lily,
Brandy bottle *or*
Spatterdock

Do not confuse the common name with any form of yellow waterlily. The Nuphar, although related to the Nymphaeas, is different in that it is very vigorous and therefore invasive. It is really suited only to large, deep ponds or lakes. However, if these are the sorts of conditions you can provide, then forms of Nuphar will make excellent choices.

This plant is widespread in natural conditions, having its origins throughout the Eastern USA and the West Indies, across to North Africa, and into Eastern Europe and Asia. *Nuphar lutea* is often referred to as brandy bottle, owing both to the shape of the flowers and their 'alcoholic' scent (which some believe smells more like cats, but the good thing is that you cannot usually get that close to them). Bright yellow bottle-shaped flowers appear in summer. After the flowers fade, decorative flask-shaped seed-heads are produced.

The leaves come in two entirely different forms: under the water they are translucent, thin and feathery, while those carried floating on the water are rounded, heart-shaped and up to 30cm (12in) across.

During spring, plant the rhizomes or young plants into baskets (the larger the better). Little attention need be given after this, other than to remove dead foliage or flowers and to wash off any aphids that might be seen.

N. japonica var. *variegata* and *N. pumila variegata* are much smaller, thriving in a depth of up to 45cm (18in).

site	Best in a large pond with a 1–2.5m (3–8ft) depth of water. Full sun or partial shade
temp	Very hardy, tolerating temperatures as low as -20°C (-4°F)
general care	Plant up the rhizomes or young plants in baskets during spring – the bigger the baskets the better
thinning	If accessible, plants should be divided every spring, with the older sections discarded
pests & diseases	Aphids can cause a few problems but apart from this, these plants are relatively trouble free

Nuphar lutea

	SPRING	SUMMER	AUTUMN	WINTER	height (cm)	spread (cm)	flower colour	
Nuphar japonica var. *variegata*	🖐🖐🖐	● ● ● ●			10	200		Leaves have brown and light green markings
N. lutea	🖐🖐🖐	● ● ●			15	200+		Very invasive
N. pumila variegata	🖐🖐🖐	● ● ●			10	200		Leaves have brown and cream markings

🖐 planting　● flowering

Flowering Water Plants

Nymphaea
Waterlilies

There are numerous waterlily cultivars, however most grow too big for the small pond. It is for this reason that in the early 1900s the French hybridist Latour-Marliac, among others, devoted himself to the breeding of newer and better miniature or dwarf varieties, some of which are classed under the category known as the Pygmaea hybrids (*see below*) and others as 'small' or 'compact'.

Generally, the native species of Nymphaea are not the best for most ponds, because they are not as ornamental and do not perform as reliably as the named cultivars.

All hardy Nymphaea are day-flowerers, usually opening their blooms around 9am, and closing around 4pm. On dark, cloudy days they may not open at all. Unless the plants are overcrowded, the flowers usually rest on the water surface. They come in a wide range of colours, from the purest of whites to the darkest of reds.

site	Best in a still pond in full sun – flowering may be reduced in even light shade
temp	Waterlilies are very hardy, surviving temperatures at -20°C (-4°F)
general care	Plant any time from mid-spring to mid-summer. Site newly bought containerised waterlilies straight away
thinning	Divide every three or four years during mid- to late spring
pests & diseases	Aphids, waterlily beetle, waterlily brown spot and leaf miners can cause problems to these plants

Pygmy waterlilies

Pygmy waterlilies are excellent for sinks, troughs or ponds where the water is no deeper than 30cm (12in). Most of these will grow well in just 10cm (4in) of water or even in the deeper marginal shelves of a larger pond.

There are two notes of caution when it comes to growing these small varieties. The first is the likelihood of the plants freezing in winter: despite being hardy, the plants grow in very shallow water, which in the harshest of winters can freeze solid. Provide the plants with sufficient depth to ensure that the rhizomes remain unfrozen during the coldest spells. If this is not possible, protect them by lifting the plants in mid-autumn and keeping them in water in a frost-free place until planting time again.

The second warning concerns the fact that these small waterlilies are perfect for growing in contained water features, such as a barrel, tub or sink. There is a temptation, however, for many of us to fit a small ornamental fountain or a regular drip-drip feature of some kind. All waterlilies, of whatever size, dislike moving water around their leaves and stems (which suppresses flowering), and this problem can be exacerbated in a container.

Nymphaea 'Pygmaea Alba' (also sold as *N. tetragona*) has white, single blooms with golden yellow stamens. The leaves are deep green, dark red beneath, and tiny. It is the only waterlily that can be grown in an aquarium with any degree of success. 'Pygmaea Rubra', meanwhile, has blood red single flowers with orange stamens. The purplish-green leaves have reddish undersides. Slightly larger is 'Pygmaea Rubis', with single, wine red flowers and yellow stamens.

Nymphaea 'Pygmaea Alba'

	SPRING	SUMMER	AUTUMN	WINTER	height (cm)	spread (cm)	flower colour	
Nymphaea 'Pygmaea Alba'	🖐🖐🖐	●●			15	45-50	⬜	Can be grown in an aquarium
N. 'Pygmaea Helvola'	🖐🖐🖐	●●			15	60	⬜	Often seen as *N. x helvola*
N. 'Pygmaea Rubis'	🖐🖐🖐	●●			20	60	⬛	Single flowers
N. 'Pygmaea Rubra'	🖐🖐🖐	●●			15	60	⬛	Reddish tinge to underside of leaves

 planting   *flowering*

Small waterlilies

These waterlilies are ideal for the smaller pond or large container water features, with a water depth of 10–30cm (4–12in). They generally have a spread, when mature, of around 30–60cm (1–2ft).

Known as a chameleon or changeable waterlily, *Nymphaea* 'Aurora' produces semi-double flowers of mid-yellow, gradually changing through orange to red. This can happen over several days, so a number of different colours may be seen at the same time, adding to its appeal. Its stamens are yellow, and it has mid-green leaves with attractive mottled and marbled patterns. It is best in a depth of 30–45cm (12–18in) and can spread to 12–24in (30–60cm). 'Aurora' is ideal for a tub garden container.

The fragrant blooms of 'Paul Hariot', on the other hand, are semi-double yellow, turning reddish-orange with yellow stamens. The mid-green leaves have a purplish flecking.

Of the warmer colours, 'Froebelii' is vivid red, single, with yellow stamens and mid-green leaves. 'Graziella' is coppery-red, single, with orange stamens and pale green leaves with purple flecking. 'Maurice Laydeker' is a single, deep wine red with white flecks on the outer petals, and yellow stamens.

A very popular and old variety is 'Johann Pring', which produces deep pink, single flowers, with stamens in two rings – the inner ones are pale orange, and the outer ones deep pink.

Nymphaea 'Froebelii'

	SPRING	SUMMER	AUTUMN	WINTER	height (cm)	spread (cm)	flower colour	
Nymphaea 'Aurora'	🖐🖐🖐	⚫⚫			15	60		Colour changes as it ages
N. 'Froebelii'	🖐🖐🖐	⚫⚫			15	60		One of the most vivid reds
N. 'Graziella'	🖐🖐🖐	⚫⚫			15	60		Leaves with attractive markings
N. 'Johann Pring'	🖐🖐🖐	⚫⚫			15	60		Bright green leaves
N. 'Maurice Laydecker'	🖐🖐🖐	⚫⚫			15	60		One of the deepest coloured waterlilies
N. 'Paul Hariot'	🖐🖐🖐	⚫⚫			15	60		Fragrant flowers

 planting   ⚫ flowering

Compact waterlilies

These waterlilies are ideal for small ponds or large contained water features, with a water depth of 30–60cm (12–24in). They generally have a spread, when mature, of some 60–100cm (2–3ft).

There are a number of very good yellows, including 'Odorata Sulphurea Grandiflora' (yellow, semi-double, yellow stamens, mid-green leaves with brownish markings).

'Sioux' (yellow, turning orange then rich red, semi-double, yellow stamens, greenish bronze leaves with brown mottling), and 'Solfatare' (yellow, turning orange-yellow and then red, single, yellow stamens, dark green leaves with purple blotches and spots).

Nymphaea 'Albatross'

One of the most widely seen compact waterlilies is 'James Brydon', crimson, semi-double to double, fragrant, red stamens with gold tips, dark purple-green leaves with maroon flecks.

In the 'compact' category there are only a few white forms, and the best is generally regarded to be 'Albatross'. Its pure white, single, flowers hold golden stamens, and the leaves are purplish, gradually turning deep green.

Nymphaea 'Odorata'

	SPRING			SUMMER			AUTUMN			WINTER			height (cm)	spread (cm)	flower colour	
Nymphaea 'Albatross'	🌱	🌱	🌱	●	●	●							20	100	⬜	Purple leaves turn to green
N. 'Brakeleyi Rosea'	🌱	🌱	🌱	●	●	●							20	100	◻	Fragrant flowers
N. 'Comanche'	🌱	🌱	🌱	●	●	●							20	100	◻	Semi-double
N. 'Ellisiana'	🌱	🌱	🌱	●	●	●							20	100	◻	Flowers darken with age
N. 'Indiana'	🌱	🌱	🌱	●	●	●							20	100	◻	Olive green leaves with mottling
N. 'James Brydon'	🌱	🌱	🌱	●	●	●							20	100	◻	One of the most commonly seen cultivars
N. 'Laydekeri Fulgens'	🌱	🌱	🌱	●	●	●							20	100	◻	Dark green leaves with purple flecks
N. 'Laydekeri Lilacea'	🌱	🌱	🌱	●	●	●							20	100	◻	Bright yellow stamens
N. 'Laydekeri Purpurata'	🌱	🌱	🌱	●	●	●	●						20	100	◻	Long season of flowering
N. 'Odorata'	🌱	🌱	🌱	●	●	●							20	100	⬜	White and yellow flowers
N. 'Robinsoniana'	🌱	🌱	🌱	●	●	●							20	100	◻	Dark green leaves with darker flecking
N. 'Sioux'	🌱	🌱	🌱	●	●	●							20	100	◻	Semi-double
N. 'Solfatare'	🌱	🌱	🌱	●	●	●							20	100	◻	Single

🌱 *planting* ● *flowering*

Large waterlilies

Perhaps the most dramatic of all waterlilies are the larger cultivars, which are more suited, by definition, to larger ponds – or even lakes. These require a planting depth of 45–80cm (18–32in), and produce a spread of leaves, when established, of up to 2.4m (8ft). Because these plants are usually sited in ponds some distance from the edges, maintaining them can sometimes be a problem. Wading in to the pond, or reaching out with makeshift cutting tools (such as a razor blade attached to a bamboo cane), are often the only options available.

Nymphaea 'Gladstoneana' is a true giant of a waterlily: double, white, fragrant flowers hold golden-yellow stamens. Another variety, 'Mrs Richmond', is an equally impressive large waterlily, with double pale pink flowers turning to red, and yellow stamens.

Nymphaea 'Gladstoneana'

Tropical waterlilies

Waterlilies from tropical climates have an entirely different appeal to the hardy form discussed above. Many are highly fragrant (and have been used in the making of perfumes). They are important enough to deserve a mention, but they are really only suitable for growing under conservatory conditions, or outside in hot, humid countries.

They tend to be more floriferous than the hardy types, and the most common flower colour is blue. They can also be very vigorous, often reaching 2.4m (8ft) in a season.

Planting should only take place when the water has reached a temperature of 21°C (70°F).

Nymphaea 'Perry's Pink'

	SPRING	SUMMER	AUTUMN	WINTER	height (cm)	spread (cm)	flower colour	
Nymphaea 'Conqueror'	🛠🛠🛠	● ● ●			20	240	■	Produces masses of flowers
N. 'Escarboucle'	🛠🛠🛠	● ● ●			20	240	■	Semi-double and fragrant
N. 'Gladstoniana'	🛠🛠🛠	● ● ●			20	240	□	Double and fragrant
N. 'Perry's Pink'	🛠🛠🛠	● ● ●			20	240	■	Light pink blooms
N. 'Mrs Richmond'	🛠🛠🛠	● ● ●			20	240	■	Leaves have slightly wavy edges
N. 'Rose Arey'	🛠🛠🛠	● ● ●			20	240	■	Purple leaves turning green
N. 'William Falconer'	🛠🛠🛠	● ● ●			20	240	■	Flowers can be single or semi-double

 planting   ● flowering

Nymphoides peltata

Water fringe

Originally from the waterways of Europe and Asia, this plant has now become naturalized throughout the USA. Some older gardeners still refer to this as the 'poor man's waterlily' owing to the pretty, almost buttercup-like flowers being held on stems over attractive leathery waterlily-like leaves. Alternative common names are the fringed waterlily, and the yellow floating heart.

Curiously, the yellow blooms do not actually look like waterlilies. Each flower is 5cm (2in) across, and the petals have frilled edges, giving them some distinction. Sadly, the blooms only last for one day. However, a large area of water fringe will produce so many flowers that there will always be a few open on each day of the normal flowering season, from mid-summer to early autumn.

Heart-shaped, waxy, deciduous leaves 10cm (4in) across, float on the surface of the water. The leaves are slightly mottled

site	Will grow at its best in a large pond in full sun or light shade
temp	An extremely hardy plant, surviving temperatures at -20°C (-4°F)
general care	Plant during spring; remove dead foliage in autumn before it sinks and pollutes the water
thinning	This is a very invasive species. Lift and divide plants each spring
pests & diseases	Aphids can cause a few problems but apart from this, these plants are relatively trouble free

Nymphoides peltata 'Bennettii'

light and dark green, with purple undersides.

Plant rhizomes or young plants in spring. The ideal water depth is 45cm (18in). Unless you have a very large pond, make sure you contain them within planting baskets.

The plant produces roots from virtually every leaf node, which is both how it spreads and why it is considered to be invasive. It is advisable to lift plants out of the pond and divide them every spring.

Although the straight species is most commonly seen, the form *Nymphoides peltata* 'Bennettii' is becoming more widely available. It produces slightly larger flowers than the species, but lacks some of the attractive leaf mottling.

This plant is suitable for both the decorative pool and wildlife water garden.

	SPRING	SUMMER	AUTUMN	WINTER	height (cm)	spread (cm)	flower colour	
Nymphoides peltata	🌱 🌱 🌱	⚬ ⚬ ⚬	⚬		10	100+		Heart-shaped waxy leaves
N. peltata 'Bennettii'	🌱 🌱 🌱	⚬ ⚬ ⚬	⚬		10	100+		Larger flowers

 planting   ⚬ flowering

Orontium aquaticum

Golden club

This is a one-species plant, originally from the Atlantic side of North America. It is a slow-growing hardy perennial aquatic needing to be in full view so that the magnificent flower spikes with deep yellow markings can be fully appreciated. Orontium is an accommodating plant and can be grown centrally in a small pool – where it can be truly spectacular – or near the edge as a marginal in larger ponds.

Orontium aquaticum is a member of the arum family, the flowers of which all follow along the same lines: a large spade-like bract, called the 'spathe', surrounds a finger-like flower spike called the 'spadix'. In this plant, however, the spathe is a small, insignificant structure at the base of the long white spadix. These spikes – which appear from mid-spring to early summer – each have golden tips similar to lit candles, and are held just above water level. Small green fruits develop under the surface of the water when the spikes fade.

The lance-shaped leaves are deciduous and almost succulent in appearance. They are dark purplish-green beneath and silvery on top. In shallow water the leaves form an erect clump, but can be floating or partly submerged elsewhere.

In ponds use aquatic baskets; ordinary (but deep) garden soil is suitable if Orontium is to be grown as a marginal

site	A position in the full sun or very light shade is best	
temp	Fairly hardy, tolerating winter temperatures as low as -15°C (5°F)	
general care	Plant young plants in spring, or dormant rhizomes in winter. Can grow 30cm (12in) high and 60cm (24in) spread	
thinning	Divide overcrowded plants in summer, after flowering has finished	
pests & diseases	This plant is relatively trouble free. Pests and diseases do not usually cause them any problems	

plant. Keep more invasive plants away from Orontium. In autumn, remove any dead foliage, and apply a mulch of leaf mould to land-grown plants. Orontiums seldom require dividing. They should only be disturbed if they are being propagated, or if the baskets in which they are growing have become crowded.

To propagate Orontium, sow ripe seeds in summer, in moist soil or under glass. Rhizomes can be easily divided in spring; each segment should have a node, from which new growth will emerge. Cuttings taken from the roots, in spring, can also be successful.

Orontium aquaticum

Persicaria amphibia

Willow grass *or* Amphibious bistort

Willow grass is not often seen, but is certainly worth searching for from specialist nurseries. Persicaria is the new name given to many former members of the 150-species strong Polygonum genus.

Most species under this original classification were best known for their potential to become weed-like (as demonstrated by the devastating Japanese knotweed, *Polygonum japonicum*), and for their rapid growth rate, (such as the mile-a-minute vine, *Polygonum baldschuanicum*). Some years ago, botanists decided that the genus needed to be broken up, and several species were given the new name of Persicaria.

As the full Latin name of our subject of interest here suggests, *Persicaria amphibia* is amphibious: it will grow on land and in water, and is found growing naturally in waterways throughout the temperate regions of the northern hemisphere. On land it is as rampant as many of its contemporaries. In the water, however, it is altogether more submissive. It is also ideal as an insect habitat and also produces good wildfowl food in its seeds, making it an excellent plant for the wildlife water garden.

Persicaria amphibia

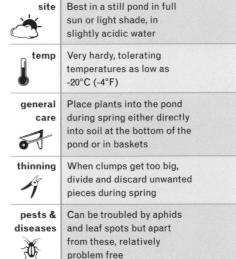
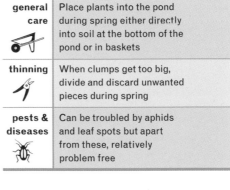

site	Best in a still pond in full sun or light shade, in slightly acidic water
temp	Very hardy, tolerating temperatures as low as -20°C (-4°F)
general care	Place plants into the pond during spring either directly into soil at the bottom of the pond or in baskets
thinning	When clumps get too big, divide and discard unwanted pieces during spring
pests & diseases	Can be troubled by aphids and leaf spots but apart from these, relatively problem free

Tiny pinkish or reddish flowerheads appear on spikes from mid-summer to mid-autumn.

The leaves are elongated, oval, mid-green and deciduous. In deepish water they float, whilst in shallow waters the leaves may point upwards, although never vertical. It grows best in around 45cm (18in) of water; the shallower the water, the more invasive the plant becomes.

Plant out young plants in spring, either directly into the soil at the bottom of the pond, or in planting baskets. Remove dead foliage at any time.

To propagate *Persicaria amphibia*, divide plants in spring, or sow fresh seeds into mud in submerged pots.

Pontederia cordata

Pickerel weed

Often regarded as the best blue flowered aquatic plant, this is a native of North America. It is called the 'pickerel' weed after the fact that various types of pike hide among its dense growth in the wild. It is considered a worthy plant for both the pond and the hardy herbaceous border. Sited in groups in deeper water, it is quite undemanding, coming into its own when most other flowers have finished.

Although perfectly acceptable as a marginal plant, pickerel weed can become invasive. It is, therefore, best treated as a deep-water aquatic, where it can be grown and 'controlled' in baskets.

The blooms are tiny, pale blue to purple, massed tightly on cylindrical spikes, appearing from mid-summer to early autumn. Not all of the flowers on a spike open at the same time, which can give spikes a 'moth-eaten' look. But when grown in sufficient numbers, there is a very splendid mass effect. The deciduous leaves are deep green, spear- or heart-shaped, held on strong stalks rising from the water.

The white-flowered form is worth growing; look for *Pontederia cordata alba*. The variety *P. cordata* var. *lancifolia* has slimmer leaves, and is a slightly taller plant.

In spring, set out young plants 30cm (12in) apart, in small isolated groups directly into soil, or in baskets (to limit their spread). The ideal depth of water for aquatically grown Pontederia is 10–38cm (4–15in). Remove dead foliage as it appears.

For best appearance, several plants should be grown together, so a medium to large pond is recommended for these plants; do not grow Pontederia in water barrels, sinks or other containers.

Plants are hardy, surviving the winter provided the crowns are below the ice. If grown in soil at the pond edge, protect the crowns in winter with a mulch of bracken or straw. To propagate, during autumn sow the fresh seeds in submerged pots under glass. Alternatively, divide mature plants in late spring.

Pontederia cordata alba

site	Performs best in full sun, in moist soil down to a 38cm (15in) depth of water
temp	Very hardy, tolerating temperatures as low as -20°C (-4°F)
general care	In spring, set out young plants 30cm (12in) apart either directly into soil at the bottom of the pond or baskets
thinning	Divide overgrown or mature plants during late spring
pests & diseases	Relatively trouble free. Pests and diseases do not usually cause any problems

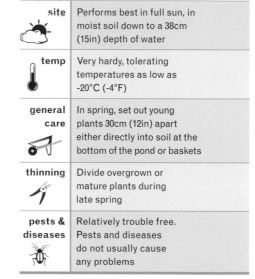

Pontederia cordata

	SPRING	SUMMER	AUTUMN	WINTER	height (cm)	spread (cm)	flower colour	
Pontederia cordata	🌱 🌱 🌱	● ● ●	●		75	45	▨	Grow several plants together
P. cordata alba	🌱 🌱 🌱	● ● ●	●		75	45	☐	Can be invasive in time
P. cordata var. lancifolia	🌱 🌱 🌱	● ● ●	●		80	50	▨	Has slimmer leaves

🌱 *planting*   ● *flowering*

Sparganium erectum

Branched
burr reed

This plant is a common sight growing wild on the edges of river banks and ditches throughout Europe, from the Arctic Circle downwards, through north Africa, Asia, the western Himalayas, Japan, north America and even south-east Australia. Although appearing like a reed, technically it is not one at all.

Sparganium erectum makes a good garden plant, performing better if sited in deeper water rather than in the shallows or pond margins. In summer, small pale green flowers appear, massed in rounded spiky heads or burrs. The female flowers are larger and positioned towards the bases of the branched stalks. The deciduous leaves, that are semi-deciduous in milder areas, are long, green and grass-like.

If you have a very large pool, plant young specimens directly into the soil, otherwise into planting baskets. Avoid planting the burr reed in shallow water where it will soon spread and become a menace. All planting is best carried out in spring. The best position is in full sun, but moderate shade is acceptable. Little on-going care is needed, but dead stems and leaves should be removed in autumn.

The best way to propagate Sparganium is to divide the plants in spring. An alternative method is to sow fresh seeds into mud in submerged pots.

Depending on the depth of water – ideally set at around 30cm (12in) – the leaves may reach up to 1.5m (5ft) after three years.

Sparganium erectum

Normally *Sparganium erectum* is the only species to be seen, but it may sometimes be sold under its alternative but less correct name *Sparganium ramosum*.

Sparganium erectum

site	Grows best in a pond that is situated in full sun or light shade
temp	Very hardy, tolerating temperatures as low as -20°C (-4°F)
general care	Plant during spring directly into the soil or into baskets; remove dead stems and leaves in autumn
thinning	Lift and divide plants during spring, annually or every alternate year
pests & diseases	Relatively trouble free. Pests and diseases do not usually cause any problems

Marginal Plants

Some confusion exists over the true definition of a marginal plant. Does it permanently have its roots in soil under water? Or are its roots just in permanently moist soil? Perhaps it is a plant that has its roots in soil that is wet or under water, but which also has periods of being dry! To offer a little clarity we have defined marginals as plants that grow at the very edge of the water, regardless of the moisture content of the soil in which they are growing.

Then there are plants that grow alongside a stream (naturally occurring or man-made). Few streams have a constant level of water; fluctuations lead to wet, occasionally wet or dry soils, and so plants growing here must be able to withstand the changing conditions.

This means that the plants discussed here will require a wide range of habitat and soil conditions (from being permanently under water to semi-dry). However, there is a danger that marginal plants will graduate, almost imperceptibly, into bog garden plants, which are featured later in this book.

Some marginals contribute to water quality by removing excess nutrients through their roots, but the main reason marginals are grown is that they improve the appearance of the pond. They break up the hard-line edges of a formal pond, and they are regularly grown to disguise awkward pond edges (exposed black liner, or cracked concrete).

The classic example of a marginal plant is the marsh marigold, or golden kingcup (*Caltha palustris*); its bright yellow spring flowers are some of the most long-awaited. No water garden should be without one or two of these. Then there is the ubiquitous arum lily (*Zantedeschia aethiopica*), with its bright white summer spathes illuminating a dark corner.

Some deep water irises have already been discussed (pages 66–70), but there are many other types that are suited either to the pond margins or the bog garden. As they are reasonably interchangeable, they are all included on pages 120–121, in our section on bog garden plants.

Acorus
Sweet flag

The leaves of this popular hardy herbaceous plant were often used to cover the floors of castles before the introduction of carpets; the 'sweet' part of the name refers to the pleasing aroma – reminiscent of cinnamon or citrus – which comes from the leaves when they are crushed. The plant's rhizome also contains oil that is extracted for use in the perfume industry.

Although small, green-brown insignificant flowers are carried at the tops of the stems on mature plants during early to mid-summer, it is the foliage that is the main feature. The all-green leaves of the straight species give it the appearance of an iris, but it is in no way related. Deciduous, arching, iris-like leaves up to 2.5cm (1in) wide have a very pronounced mid-rib. In warm climates, reddish seeds are formed in mid-summer.

Its less vigorous variegated form is the one most often seen. *Acorus calamus* 'Argenteostriatus' (formerly 'Variegatus') starts with pink and cream shoots in early spring, which turn into gold and cream striped leaves.

site	Grows best in a pond which is situated in full sun or light shade
temp	Very hardy, tolerating temperatures as low as -20°C (-4°F)
general care	Feed with a slow-release pellet for aquatic plants in spring; remove dead foliage in autumn
thinning	Lift and divide plants during spring. *A. calamus* forms will need regular trimming
pests & diseases	Relatively trouble free. Pests and diseases do not usually cause any problems

A. calamus 'Argenteostriatus'

A. gramineus (referred to as the Dwarf Japanese Rush, although the plant is not technically a rush) is about a third of the size of *A. calamus*, and has vertical green and white striped grass-like leaves. It is evergreen in all but the harshest of conditions.

Forms of *A. calamus* can grow rather large, so are best suited to larger ponds. If kept in smaller ponds the plants will require regular trimming back.

In spring, plant rhizomes directly into the soil, preferably in water 8–25cm (3–10in) deep. Choose a site that is in full sun or very light shade.

To propagate, which is very easy, simply cut off a piece of healthy rhizome in spring and plant it immediately in mud at the recommended depth.

	SPRING	SUMMER	AUTUMN	WINTER	height (cm)	spread (cm)	flower colour	
Acorus calamus	🌱🌱🌱	✺✺			120	75		Best for larger ponds
A. calamus 'Argenteostriatus'	🌱🌱🌱	✺✺			95	75		Gold and cream striped leaves
A. gramineus	🌱🌱🌱	✺✺			40	35		Undemanding, low-growing plant

 planting   flowering

Butomus umbellatus

Flowering rush *or* Water gladiolus

This not a true rush despite, in some respects, resembling one. It is perfectly at home in the shallow waters of a still pool, and a mature plant in full flower is a sight to behold. Some people in parts of temperate Asia where it originates bake and eat the nutritious rhizomes.

During mid- to late summer 30 or more small rose-pink blooms are held in rounded heads some 2.5cm (1in) across. It rarely sets set in colder climates. The leaves are narrow, grass-like and purplish when young, gradually turning green.

The white-flowered variety *Butomus umbellatus* 'Schneeweibschen' is excellent,

site	Grows best in a pond which is situated in full sun or light shade
temp	Very hardy, surviving temperatures as low as -20°C (-4°F)
general care	Plant these in a basket during the spring; remove any dead stems and leaves in autumn
thinning	Divide overgrown clumps every three or four years in spring
pests & diseases	Sometimes aphids can be a problem during the summer months, but otherwise fairly trouble free

Butomus umbellatus

although there are not usually so many flowers per plant. Then there is the deeper pink *B. umbellatus* 'Rosenrot' which, when viewed close-up, is stunningly beautiful. However, this variety may be slightly more difficult to find.

During spring, plant in a basket containing a high level of clay or at least a heavy loam soil. A sand or peat-based mixture will not work so well. Set in a water depth of 2.5–15cm (1–6in), preferably in a position that receives full sun for the best growing conditions. Cut down all growth in autumn.

To propagate, divide overgrown clumps every couple of years in spring. Alternatively, sow seeds under glass in autumn – but be warned that the germination rates are usually poor, so you could be disappointed.

	SPRING	SUMMER	AUTUMN	WINTER	height (cm)	spread (cm)	flower colour	
Butomus umbellatus	🌱 🌱 🌱	● ●			90	60		Use heavy or clay soil
B. umbellatus 'Rosenrot'	🌱 🌱 🌱	● ●			90	60		Difficult to find
B. umbellatus 'Schneeweibschen'	🌱 🌱 🌱	● ●			90	60		Fewer flowers but a brilliant white

🌱 *planting*　● *flowering*

Calla palustris

Bog arum

This extremely hardy perennial is perfectly at home either as a marginal plant or as a shallow water aquatic. It is ideal for concealing the sides of a man-made pond – its stout rhizomes eventually colonising the shallows and supporting a lush dense carpet of leaves. Arguably, the autumn berries – which are poisonous, however – are even more attractive looking than the flowers.

The flowers appear in late spring and early summer. They are tiny and yellow-green, studded on a cylindrical spike enclosed by a prominent bright white funnel-shaped, arum-like spathe. Water snails are thought to be instrumental creatures in pollination of the flowers. Broadly heart-shaped, glossy rich green and thick leaves are carried on long stalks growing from strong creeping rhizomes. Normally only this single species is available.

Planting should take place during spring, placing pieces of the rhizomes 23cm (9in) apart directly into wet soil or in baskets. Choose a position in full sun or light shade, in wet soil at the edge of larger ponds, or in shallow water to a depth of 20cm (8in).

If planted in baskets, these plants will not spread so rapidly and are easier to keep in check. Cut down dead foliage in autumn and winter. Keep the plants healthy by dividing the larger clumps every four or five years.

To propagate, divide the rhizomes in spring, either transplanting the divisions

site	Grows best in a pond which is situated in full sun or light shade
temp	Very hardy, tolerating temperatures to -20°C (-4°F) or more
general care	Plant during spring in wet soil or in baskets; remove dead stems and leaves in autumn
thinning	Lift and divide plants during spring, every four or five years
pests & diseases	Relatively trouble free. Pests and diseases do not usually cause any problems

directly into the pond or by starting them into growth in trays of mud under glass and then planting out. The berries can be sown when ripe, in pots of wet soil.

The arum lily (*Zantedeschia aethiopica*) is formerly *Calla aethiopica* and is often referred to as the calla lily; it is a close relation, and an extremely valuable marginal and bog garden plant in its own right (see page 101).

Calla palustris originates throughout Northern Europe, Siberia and North America; in Lapland, the rhizomes of the bog arum are dried, ground and processed to be used as a kind of flour for baking in Finnish 'missebroed'.

Calla palustris

Caltha palustris

Marsh marigold
or Golden
kingcup

This aquatic 'buttercup' is one of the most familiar and loved plants for pondside planting. With deep golden flowers and large, rounded leaves, much of its appeal derives from the neatness of habit: Caltha does not become straggly and unkempt in the way so many marginals do.

From mid-spring to early summer, golden yellow, waxy buttercup-like blooms appear, proud of the glossy, dark green deciduous leaves. These leaves are more or less rounded, and carried on long stalks.

During early spring, Caltha should be planted directly into the soil at the edge of the pond. It prefers a position in full sun, but grows very well in medium shade; it is often found naturally in waterlogged woodland soils. There is little maintenance required, just to remove dead foliage when seen and give a general tidy-up in the autumn.

If you have a small pond you can only really grow single plants. If planting directly into soil under water, there should be a maximum water depth of 15cm (6in). For a more impressive display, plant three or more plants together, about 30cm (12in) apart (obviously the size of the pond will dictate whether this is possible).

To propagate, sow fresh seed in late summer or early autumn in wet soil. Alternatively, divide the spreading roots of larger clumps in summer, after the flowers have faded.

Although most gardeners grow the single-flowered species, there are also the tightly double-flowered *Caltha palustris* 'Flore Pleno', which is free-flowering, and the single-flowered white form, *C. palustris* var. *alba*. This latter plant is slightly more compact and therefore ideal for smaller ponds. *C. leptosepala* is also better placed for small ponds; it has rather dainty star-like, golden-centred white flowers. A larger and more vigorous form of *C. palustris* is available, and as if to emphasise its stature, it is called *C. palustris* var. *palustris*.

Caltha palustris

site	Grows best in a pond which is situated in full sun or light shade	
temp	Very hardy, tolerating temperatures as low as -20°C (-4°F)	
general care	Plant during spring directly into the soil at the edge of the pond; remove dead stems and leaves in autumn	
thinning	Lift and divide crowded plants in summer after it has flowered	
pests & diseases	Sometimes aphids and mildew can pose a few problems, but otherwise fairly trouble free	

	SPRING	SUMMER	AUTUMN	WINTER	height (cm)	spread (cm)	flower colour	
Caltha leptosepala					60	50		More compact than *C. palustris*
C. palustris					60	50		If you can, plant three or more together
C. palustris var. *alba*					60	50		Single flowers
C. palustris 'Flore Pleno'					60	50		Tightly double flowered
C. palustris var. *palustris*					75	60		A larger, more vigorous form

planting   flowering

Cotula

Brass buttons *or*
Golden buttons

This is a pretty little plant, grown either as a short-lived tender perennial (in warmer countries), but more often as an annual. Fortunately, it usually produces many seeds when the flowers fade, and these help to ensure a further crop of plants for the following year. It is originally from the waterways of South Africa and southern Asia.

The fine, shiny, light green leaves, which are also aromatic, make the plant ideally suited to hiding the edges of ponds and bare soil in containers. From late spring to early autumn Cotula will be covered with masses of small, brilliant golden button-shaped blooms, borne upwards from the foliage.

Plant young plants or transplant self-sown seedlings in late spring. A position in full sun is best, in water 0–10cm (0–4in)

site	Grows best in a pond which is situated in full sun at all times
temp	The severest temperatures tolerated by this plant are in the region of -10°C (14°F)
general care	Plant during spring in water 0–10cm (0–4in) deep; remove dead flowers to prevent seeding
thinning	Remove plants at end of year, allowing self-sown seedlings to replace them
pests & diseases	Relatively trouble free. Pests and diseases do not usually cause any problems

Cotula coronopifolia

deep. Because of its propensity to self-sow, Cotula will, if left to its own devices in a mild or sheltered garden, colonize a fairly large area quite rapidly. Control the self-seeding by removing old flowers, before the seeds have time to form and drop. Remove excess or any frost-damaged foliage to prevent it from falling in and polluting the water.

To propagate, simply allow it to self-seed and transplant the seedlings to better places as soon as they are large enough to move. Alternatively, sow seeds under glass in spring, pricking them out into small pots, or take stem cuttings from late spring to early summer.

Although there are several other species of Cotula, only *Cotula coronopifolia* is considered to be truly aquatic and is thus the only one suited to water gardens.

	SPRING	SUMMER	AUTUMN	WINTER	height (cm)	spread (cm)	flower colour	
Cotula coronopifolia	🌱🌱🌱	● ● ● ●	●		20	35		Best treated as an annual
C. pyrethrifolia	🌱🌱🌱	● ● ● ●	●		20	30		May be found under *Leptinella pyrethrifolia*
C. squalida	🌱🌱🌱	● ● ● ●	●		15	45		May be found under *Leptinella squalida*

 planting ● *flowering*

Eriophorum
Cotton grass

This is an elegant genus of hardy perennial sedge. Native to high-altitude pools, streams, marshes and moorlands with acid soils, throughout the Northern hemisphere, it is even seen growing in Arctic regions. Suited both to the bog garden and the margins of a pond, it is extremely slow growing, and is quite unmistakeable in summer when its seedheads form cottonwool-like tufts.

Although not the easiest of plants to grow in low-altitude water gardens, it is certainly worth trying. The small insignificant blooms with bright yellow anthers appear in early to mid-spring. They are followed in summer by brown seedpods, which, when they split open they expose attractive tufts of white silky hairs. These are the main feature of the plant, and are most attractive when seen en masse. If the 'tufts' are picked when at their best, they dry and last well for floral decoration indoors.

Allow the flower stems to die down naturally each year. The leaves are in shades from olive green to reddish brown, depending on the situation. They are long, slim and drooping, in clumps.

Choose a position in full sun or light shade, in wet peaty acid soil at the edge of larger ponds, or in shallow water no deeper than 10cm (4in). Plant 23cm (9in) apart directly into wet soil or into baskets. Eriophorum is an undemanding plant, as

site	Grows best in a pond which is situated in full sun or light shade
temp	Very hardy, tolerating temperatures as low as -20°C (-4°F)
general care	Plant in containers during the spring; remove dead stems and leaves in autumn
thinning	Lift and divide plants every four years; containers will prevent undue spreading
pests & diseases	Relatively trouble free. Pests and diseases do not usually cause any problems

long as it has acid soil and water. If growing in the bog garden as opposed to growing in water, mulch in spring (particularly if the soil is likely to dry out), and feed with a general fertilizer in spring while young. Keep the plants healthy by dividing the larger clumps every four or five years. If space permits, cotton grass should be planted in bold drifts at the edge of a wildlife pond to create a natural effect.

To propagate, divide larger clumps in spring; either transplant the divisions directly or start them into growth in trays of mud under glass and then plant them out. Alternatively, sow seeds in wet ericaceous compost under glass in spring.

The broad-leafed cotton grass (*Eriophorum latifolium*) is slightly larger and tolerates some lime content in the soil and water but seems to have a shorter life-span.

Eriophorum angustifolium

		SPRING	SUMMER	AUTUMN	WINTER	height (cm)	spread (cm)	flower colour	
Eriophorum angustifolium						60	100+		If there is room, plant in bold drifts
E. latifolium						75	100+		Produces broader leaves

🌱 *planting*   ● *flowering*

Houttuynia cordata

Orange peel plant

This is a vigorous and easily grown semi-evergreen plant for the water's edge or bog garden. It makes attractive ground cover and can become invasive unless confined in some way. 'Chameleon' outsells any of the other forms and its brightly coloured leaves never fail to make a talking point. The common name of orange peel plant is due to the citrus-like smell one gets when the foliage, stems or roots are crushed.

In early summer small, white, four-petalled flowers appear on short stalks above the leaves. These flowers are attractive, with heart-shaped green-blue leaves.

   'Chameleon' (which can also be found wrongly named as 'Tricolor' or 'Variegata') is a recent man-made hybrid. Here the flowers pale to insignificance when compared to the foliage. The leaves are boldly variegated in shades of pink, yellow, green, cream and white. There are as many gardeners in favour of this plant as there are who would not even think of growing it. Its leaves are, to some, gaudy and unnecessary, while to others they are magnificently ornate. The form 'Flore Pleno' has double flowers.

   Plant Houttuynia during the spring or autumn, directly into the soil at the edge of the pond, or in baskets to restrain root spread. It prefers a position in partial shade, but will comfortably tolerate either full sun or

Houttuynia cordata 'Chameleon'

	site	These plants perform best when grown in partial shade
	temp	Very hardy, tolerating temperatures as low as -20°C (-4°F)
	general care	Plant during spring in baskets or directly into soil; remove dead stems, flowers and leaves as they appear
	thinning	Lift and divide plants during spring every four or five years
	pests & diseases	Can be troubled by aphids and leaf spots but apart from these, relatively problem free

Houttuynia cordata

shade. Planting should be into wet soil or directly into shallow water, no deeper than 10cm (4in). Remove dead or fading foliage and generally tidy up in the autumn. To protect soil-grown plants from frost, mulch with compost in the autumn. Clumps should be divided every four or five years. Divide the spreading roots of larger clumps in spring.

	SPRING	SUMMER	AUTUMN	WINTER	height (cm)	spread (cm)	flower colour	
Houttuynia cordata					30	45		Prefers a position in partial shade
H. cordata 'Chameleon'					30	45		Brightly coloured leaves
H. cordata 'Flore Pleno'					30	45		Has double flowers

 planting   flowering

Hypericum elodeoides

Marsh St John's wort

The hypericum is most familiar as a long-lived shrub; sometimes these are worthy garden plants, and sometimes they are more at home on roadside verges or scrubland. However, this small, creeping species from Western Europe is happiest in mud or water 0–8cm (0–3in) deep. This is the only aquatic hypericum, and may be seen under an often-used incorrect name, *Hypericum elodes*.

Hypericum elodeoides is a very good plant for concealing the edges of pond liners. Small, yellow trumpet flowers appear at the tips of the stems from mid-summer to early autumn. The leaves are small, oval and woolly, pale green to green-grey.

A sunny spot certainly brings out the best in this plant, but it will also tolerate light to medium shade. Planting can take place in spring or autumn and it is best planted in small groups of three or five, if you have the room. Because it is not large, you may be forgiven for thinking that a small pond is the ideal home for Hypericum, but it is perhaps best used as a small contribution to a massed planting around a medium sized pond, or larger.

Little in the way of cultivation is required. In spring, provide an aquatic fertilizer tablet to help sustain the plant throughout the year, and to inspire it to flower better. In the autumn remove all dead leaves and faded flowers.

site	Grows best in a pond which is situated in full sun or light shade
temp	Will tolerate as low as -20°C (-4°F) for only a short period before starting to die back
general care	Plant during spring; remove dead stems and leaves in autumn. Best planted in groups of three or five
thinning	Lift and divide plants during spring, every alternate year
pests & diseases	Relatively trouble free. Pests and diseases do not usually cause any problems

To propagate Hypericum, simply divide large clumps in alternate years in spring. Alternatively, you can try taking cuttings of soft young growth in summer and growing on.

Hypericum elodeoides

Lobelia
Cardinal flower

The mainly red-flowering aquatic Lobelias from North America are very closely related to the annual lobelias so beloved of container gardeners for their showy, blue or white overhanging flowers. The aquatic lobelias are different in almost every respect, but mainly they are hardier, taller, and not blue! Although many gardeners are tempted to grow them in ordinary garden soil, they only ever perform at their best with their roots under water.

From mid-summer to early autumn bright, rich red flowers appear in clusters on tall stalks. The glossy, narrow leaves are deep beetroot coloured.

The hybrid of *Lobelia cardinalis*, 'Queen Victoria', is stunning, with carmine flowers and blood-red leaves. Three closely related species are also worthy of mention. *Lobelia fulgens* is larger and more graceful than *L. cardinalis*, but is not frost hardy. *L. dortmanna* is a rosette-forming aquatic species with pale mauve flowers, while *L. siphillitica* is a very hardy relative with violet-blue flowers.

The best place to plant aquatic lobelias is in full sun or light shade, preferably in water 5–15cm (2–6in) deep, but most will perform well in a moist bog garden. If you live in a

Lobelia cardinalis

site	Grows best in a pond which is situated in full sun or light shade
temp	Fairly hardy, tolerating temperatures only down to -10°C (14°F)
general care	Plant during spring, in containers if in a cold climate; remove dead stems and leaves in autumn
thinning	Lift and divide plants during spring, annually or every alternate year
pests & diseases	Slugs can attack young stems and leaves, but otherwise relatively trouble free

colder area, plant them in containers and take them to a frost-free greenhouse for winter. Cut down all top growth in autumn and, if they are growing in a bog garden, cover the crowns with straw or bracken to protect them from the worst of the frosts.

To propagate, sow seeds under glass, or divide plants: both are carried out during spring. Alternatively, take soft cuttings of the plants during summer.

	SPRING	SUMMER	AUTUMN	WINTER	height (cm)	spread (cm)	flower colour	
Lobelia cardinalis	🪴🪴🪴	● ● ●	●		90	30	■	Single plant can grow in water container
L. dortmanna	🪴🪴🪴	● ● ●	●		90	30	■	Rosette-forming species
L. fulgens	🪴🪴🪴	● ● ●	●		100	40	■	A graceful relative, but not frost hardy
L. 'Queen Victoria'	🪴🪴🪴	● ● ●	●		90	30	■	Regarded by some as the best aquatic lobelia
L. siphillitica	🪴🪴	● ● ● ●	●		90	30	■	Very hardy

 planting   ● *flowering*

Mentha aquatica
Water mint

Water mint was once one of the most popular of marginal plants for the average garden. Now, mainly because of brighter and better-hybridized alternatives, this hardy herbaceous perennial is grown mostly in wildlife ponds where it is a good plant for covering the margins with its aromatic leaves and flowers that attract bees and other foragers. It can soon become invasive, however.

Flowers appear from mid- to late summer. They are characteristic of most mints: tiny, pale mauve and fragrant, in tight round clusters at the ends of shoots. Prior to flowering, leaf and stem growth can be very rapid, and you may need to control them. Once the flower shoots start to appear, however, this growth slows down.

The small, deciduous, oval, woolly or hairy leaves are dark green turning reddish purple in bright sun. Like all other mints, they are very heavily scented when crushed.

site	Grows best in a pond which is situated in full sun or light shade
temp	Very hardy, tolerating temperatures as low as -20°C (-4°F)
general care	Plant during spring in groups of three or four; remove dead stems and leaves in autumn
thinning	Lift and divide plants during spring, annually or every alternate year
pests & diseases	Like other garden mints, water mint can suffer from mildew, but it is generally not fatal

Mentha aquatica

Mentha cervina is less common, but is slightly daintier. It is low-growing and forms leafy clumps with lilac-blue flowers in late summer. Pennyroyal or brook mint (*Mentha pulegium*) is closely related; dwarf and sprawling, it also thrives in very wet soil.

Plant during spring, in groups of three or four for impact. Choose a position in full sun or light to medium shade. If planted in baskets, these plants will not spread so rapidly and are much easier to keep in check. Cut down all growth in the autumn. Keep the clumps healthy by dividing every other year.

Propagation can be carried out easily in any of three ways: by dividing up clumps, sowing seed in spring, or by taking easy-to-root stem cuttings in the spring or summer.

	SPRING	SUMMER	AUTUMN	WINTER	height (cm)	spread (cm)	flower colour	
Mentha aquatica	🌱🌱🌱	● ●			45	75		Leaves turn reddish purple in bright sun
M. cervina	🌱🌱🌱	● ●	●		30	60		Non-invasive
M. pulegium	🌱🌱🌱	● ●			5	30		Creeps over the ground along the pond edge

planting   flowering

Menyanthes trifoliata

Bog bean *or*
Marsh trefoil

The roots of this plant will grow perfectly well in the muddy soil at the sides of the pond, and they will just as happily creep out into deeper water to grow as a true aquatic. In this latter situation, however, the plant tends to be less decorative. It is a low, scrambling plant that will colonize a large area in a few years, so caution needs to be used – do not plant it in a small pond!

Bog bean, a native of several Northern European countries, is a rather unsavoury name. To many, the plant is untidy and so not particularly attractive. It is not a true 'bean' in the sense that it is not in the same family as the vegetable beans. Its smooth, shiny, bright green, pointed oval leaflets do resemble those of the broad bean, however that is where any similarity ends.

So does it have any redeeming qualities? Its main attribute is that it will cover a pond edge very well, and between mid-spring and early summer lovely white or pale pink star-shaped flowers open. The reddish flower buds are attractive in their own right. Plant it in full sun or part shade, during mid-to late autumn, or wait until spring. It grows best in a soil that is slightly acid, and a depth of water as much as 25cm (10in) will not harm the plant. Cut down dead stems in autumn.

The aerial rooted stems are ideal for propagation – remove them from the plant, pot them horizontally in a heavy loam, and submerge the pot immediately.

Alternatively, propagate by dividing larger clumps every four or five years. Do this in spring, cutting the creeping rhizomes into several rooted sections. Or you can sow seeds in pots of wet soil during late summer. The only species available is *Menyanthes trifoliata*.

site	Grows best in a pond which is situated in full sun or dappled shade
temp	Very hardy, tolerating temperatures as low as -20°C (-4°F)
general care	Plant during autumn or spring in slightly acidic soil; remove dead stems and leaves in autumn
thinning	Trim back excess and old growth or divide overgrown clumps as necessary
pests & diseases	Relatively trouble free. Pests and diseases do not usually cause any problems

Menyanthes trifoliata

Mimulus
Water musk,
Yellow musk *or*
Monkey flower

Several musk flowers make excellent plants for pond edges and margins, but they really do need room to grow (being fairly invasive and with their propensity to self-seed), so larger water gardens make the best homes.

Depending on the species and cultivar yellow, orange, red or lavender-blue flowers are carried on tall spikes. Close-up, the blooms have pronounced lips, rather like snapdragons. The leaves are small, rounded, mid-green and deciduous.

The water musk (*Mimulus luteus*) produces yellow blooms with red blotches during mid-summer. The cardinal flower (*M. cardinalis*, and not to be confused with the other cardinal flower, *Lobelia cardinalis*) has attractive downy leaves and bright red, almost scarlet flowers throughout summer. The great purple monkey flower (*M. lewisii*) carries pink to wine purple coloured flowers from early summer to mid-autumn, and the lavender musk (*M. ringens*), not surprisingly, carries pale lavender coloured flowers.

The blooms of the monkey musk (*M. moschatus*) are all-over yellow. In past centuries, this was one of the most richly perfumed garden flowers. Then, inexplicably, around the year 1914, all of the strains of this plant across the world lost much of their fragrance – and have never regained it.

Musks, most of which hail from North America, grow best in full sun in water 0–8cm (0–3in) deep – but 8–15cm (3–6in) deep in the case of *M. ringens*. Set out young plants, or transplant self-sown seedlings, in spring. Cut back

Mimulus moschatus

dead or dying stems in the autumn.

To propagate, divide overcrowded plants every two or three years; do this in spring. Take softwood cuttings in summer. Seed of some forms, such as *M. ringens*, can be sown in spring.

Mimulus lewisii

Mimulus cardinalis

site	Grows best in water gardens which are situated in full sun
temp	Very hardy, tolerating temperatures as low as -20°C (-4°F)
general care	Position young plants during the spring; cut back dead or dying stems in the autumn
thinning	Divide overcrowded plants during spring every two or three years
pests & diseases	Sometimes grey mould fungus can attack the leaves and flowers but not troubled by pests

	SPRING	SUMMER	AUTUMN	WINTER	height (cm)	spread (cm)	flower colour	
Mimulus cardinalis	planting	flowering			45	50		Do not confuse with lobelia
M. lewisii	planting	flowering	flowering		60	45		Long flowering period
M. luteus	planting	flowering	flowering		30	30		Most often seen water mimulus
M. moschatus	planting	flowering			15	30		Used to be scented
M. ringens	planting	flowering			90	50		Prefers slightly deeper water

planting · flowering

Myosotis scorpioides

Water forget-me-not

One of the main attributes of the water forget-me-not is the fact that it emerges from the shallows in spring, at a time when the pond and its immediate environment are still relatively barren. It grows easily in most situations and is very reliable. Its creeping rhizomes are not invasive; they will trail into the water, making this an ideal choice for masking pond edges. It is useful for underplanting irises and other tall aquatics.

The flowers are small, rounded, single and of an intense azure blue (with a yellow, pink or white eye). They appear from mid-spring to mid-summer. Deciduous, small, oval, bright green leaves covered in short hairs, are carried on long trailing stems.

There are several varieties worth growing. 'Pinkie' is a most attractive form with sugar-pink flowers, and 'Mermaid' has large bright blue flowers over a long season. 'Snowflakes' is a new hybrid bred in the USA, with lovely white flowers; valuable in the water garden, but it is less robust than the blue forms. A breathtaking effect can be had if this white form is grown among the blue and pink, providing a riot of colour.

Plant in spring or autumn in moist soil close to the water's edge; a depth of soil 0–15cm (0–6in) is ideal. It will tolerate a position equally well in full sun and heavy shade (some say this plant is the most shade-tolerant of all flowering aquatics). A single plant will spread to 60cm (2ft) in a year; the stems are much longer, but trail down. Cut down dead growth in autumn.

To propagate, transplant the self-sown seedlings (from species only) in spring, or take stem cuttings in summer.

Myosotis scorpioides 'Snowflakes'

Myosotis scorpioides

site	Grows in full sun, heavy shade or anything in between
temp	Very hardy, tolerating temperatures as low as -20°C (-4°F)
general care	Plant during spring or mid- to late autumn; cut down any dead growth in autumn
thinning	Cut back plants in autumn; remove unwanted plants after flowering
pests & diseases	These plants can be prone to mildew at the end of the flowering season and aphids in summer

	SPRING	SUMMER	AUTUMN	WINTER	height (cm)	spread (cm)	flower colour	
Myosotis scorpioides (syn. M. palustris)					30	60		Useful for underplanting irises
M. scorpioides 'Mermaid'					30	60		Flowers over a long season
M. scorpioides 'Pinkie'					30	60		Worth searching for
M. scorpioides 'Snowflakes'					30	60		Less robust form

 planting · flowering

Peltandra
Arrow arum

A hardy, semi-evergreen perennial originally from North America, this is a plant highly regarded for its form and structure – considered by many to be architecturally significant in the garden. Individual plants are not particularly big, but a large group can be stunning. For this reason, Peltandra is best suited to larger ponds.

The leaves are bright green, shiny, strongly veined and, most significantly of all, are arrow-shaped. Sometimes the undersides of the leaves take on a chestnut hue. When grown in deeper water, they tend to be evergreen.

Tiny greenish flowers on a short spike enclosed by a conspicuous greenish white spathe appear in early summer. Green berries follow.

Set plants out, around 30cm (12in) apart, during spring. The ideal water depth is 0–25cm (0–10in). Choose a position in full sun or very light shade. It is best to plant directly into the soil, as Peltandra does not take kindly to container growing. Remove any faded foliage in late autumn. In winter, protect plants not under water by packing straw or bracken around the crowns.

To propagate, divide the creeping rhizomes in spring.

This plant may also be found under its old names of *Peltandra undulata* or

site	Grows best in ponds situated in full sun or light shade
temp	Hardy, tolerating temperatures down to -15°C (5°F)
general care	Plant during spring directly into the soil; remove any dead stems and leaves in the autumn
thinning	Lift and divide plants during spring, annually or every alternate year
pests & diseases	Relatively trouble free. Pests and diseases do not usually cause any problems

P. sagittifolia. Sometimes the white arrow arum (*P. sagittifolia* or sometimes seen as *P. alba*) has flowers of a purer white, with red autumn berries. *P. virginica* often turns evergreen in deep water.

Peltranda sagittifolia

	SPRING	SUMMER	AUTUMN	WINTER	height (cm)	spread (cm)	flower colour	
Peltandra sagittifolia	🌱 🌱 🌱	☀ ☀			60	45	☐	Rare. May be found as *P. alba*
P. virginica	🌱 🌱 🌱	☀ ☀			60	45	☐	Often evergreen in deeper water

 planting ☀ flowering

Marginal Plants

P

Ranunculus
Spearwort

Most species in this genus are relatively invasive – think of buttercups in the lawn, for example. *Ranunculus lingua* is no different and will happily extend its creeping roots and colonize a large area. It is, therefore, not really suitable for the small pond. It redeems itself in that it is a marginal with lovely showy flowers.

Ranunculus lingua

The blooms are large, some 5cm (2in) across, golden yellow and have a sheen to them that glistens in the sun. They appear from mid-spring to early autumn. Pollinated flowers produce pretty, light green, mace-like seed heads that ripen slowly, turning to light brown.

Long, spear-shaped leaves – hence the common name – are bright green for most of the season, but are decidedly pinkish when young.

Ranunculus aquatilis is a spreading, invasive species whose flowers and stems are often submerged underwater. The lesser spearwort (*R. flammula*) is less invasive, lower-growing, and also less decorative. This form can be chosen for a small pond.

Grow marginal ranunculus in full sun or light shade, and plant them during the spring either directly into the soil or into planting baskets for siting on ledges around the pond margins.

Remove all old, dying or dead leaves and stems in autumn to avoid polluting the water. Should stems break and fall into the water, they will most probably produce roots from the leaf nodes – another way for the plant to spread.

Divide overgrown clumps, probably every three to four years, in spring.

To propagate, either divide as suggested, or sow seeds in to pots of moist compost in spring, and keep them in a shaded cold frame.

Ranunculus aquatilis

	site	Grows best in ponds which are situated in full sun or light shade
	temp	Will survive short periods at temperatures down to -20°C (-4°F)
	general care	Plant during spring; remove dead stems and leaves in autumn. If allowed to, will spread indefinitely
	thinning	Lift and divide plants during spring, whenever required or every 3–4 years
	pests & diseases	Mildew may be a problem for these plants in late summer and autumn but not troubled by pests

	SPRING	SUMMER	AUTUMN	WINTER	height (cm)	spread (cm)	flower colour	
Ranunculus aquatilis	🌱🌱🌱	●●			20	100+		Often submerged beneath the water
R. flammula	🌱🌱🌱	●●	●		20	100+		Low-growing, hugs the water surface
R. lingua	🌱🌱●	●●●●	●		90	100+		Fairly invasive

🌱 planting   ● flowering

Sagittaria

Japanese arrowhead

All sagittarias, originally from various parts of the Far East and northern Europe, are popular and attractive, even regarded by some as architectural in form. The most often seen form is *Sagittaria sagittifolia*.

The old botanical name for *Sagittaria sagittifolia* is *S. japonica*, and it may still be found under this name in nurseries. Its leaves are distinctive, particularly when combined with the flowers on the double form.

From mid- to late summer fairly large spikes of white flowers with black and red centres are produced. The male flowers are at the tops of the spikes and females below.

Elegant arrow-shaped leaves are held above the water, while long ribbons of leaves are produced under water.

site	Grows best in water gardens which are situated in full sun
temp	Very hardy, tolerating temperatures as low as -20°C (-4°F)
general care	Plant and feed during spring; cut back all growth, including dead leaves, in the autumn
thinning	Lift and divide plants during spring, every second or third year
pests & diseases	Aphids can be a problem in summer (wash them off with jets of water), and ducks can eat the tubers

The form *S. latifolia* is similar but less hardy, while *S. sagittifolia* 'Flore Pleno' produces double flowers.

When growing more than one plant, set them out 23cm (9in) apart. Plant tubers or young plants directly into the soil or simply weigh them down and drop them into the water at the pond's edge. The preferred water depth for this plant is 5–30cm (2–12in); the deeper the water, the fewer the flowers. Cut back all growth in the autumn. If practicable, feed the plants in spring.

The easiest way to propagate them is to divide them every second or third year, when they get overcrowded. Do this in spring. Also, seeds can be sown under glass in spring.

This plant has edible roots. It is sometimes referred to as the duck potato because, in large duckponds, the feathery inhabitants will attack and eat the tubers.

Sagittaria sagittifolia 'Flore Pleno'

	SPRING	SUMMER	AUTUMN	WINTER	height (cm)	spread (cm)	flower colour	
Sagittaria 'Bloomin Babe'					25	45		Flowers earlier
S. latifolia					60	45		Less hardy
S. sagittifolia					60	45		Three-petalled flowers
S. sagittifolia 'Flore Pleno'					75	45		Double flowered

 planting ⬤ flowering

Marginal Plants

S

Typha
Reed mace

This is a tall plant. The sword-shaped, blue-green leaves can reach considerable heights, and throughout summer they frame the taller brown-tipped flower stems or 'pokers'. The leaves die back in winter but the woody flower stem remains throughout the winter, looking quite attractive when covered with frost.

This is not a plant for the small – or even lined – pond as it possesses a very strong and vigorous system of pointed roots. These roots are quite capable of penetrating most flexible liners! The plant is therefore best suited to large, natural ponds and lakes. It has been successfully used in aiding the stabilization of riverbanks, as the massive root systems form a tough, dense, almost raft-like mat just below the surface.

Typha angustifolia (slender reed mace) is a graceful plant, slightly shorter in height, but otherwise similar.

On the other hand *T. minima* (miniature reed mace) is a useful plant for small ponds. Its round seed head is considerably different from the cigar-shaped heads of the other two, and the leaves are narrower. The main similarity it has with the others is its tendency to produce pointed roots.

Placing an additional layer of liner between the root system and the pond liner will certainly protect the liner, but it is a great deal of effort for a plant that is not, it must honestly be said, the most decorative of marginals!

Old foliage should be cut away during late autumn, otherwise it will die and fall into the water, polluting it. Typhas do not require feeding at any time.

To propagate, just remove a length of root system that has healthy tips and roots, pot it into a heavy loam or clay soil, and place it in the water.

Typha laxmannii

T

Marginal Plants

site	Grows best in water gardens situated in full sun or light shade
temp	Very hardy, tolerating temperatures as low as -20°C (-4°F)
general care	Plant during spring; remove dead stems and leaves in autumn. If allowed to, will spread indefinitely
thinning	Lift and divide plants during spring, annually or every alternate year
pests & diseases	Relatively trouble free. Pests and diseases do not usually cause any problems

	SPRING	SUMMER	AUTUMN	WINTER	height (cm)	spread (cm)	flower colour	
Typha angustifolia	🌱 🌱 🌱	● ● ●			170	100+		Slender and graceful
T. latifolia	🌱 🌱 🌱	● ● ●			200	100+		Loved by waterfowl
T. laxmannii	🌱 🌱 🌱	● ● ●			120	100+		A good, medium-sized reed mace
T. minima	🌱 🌱 🌱	● ● ●			60	100+		Round-headed 'pokers'
T. shuttleworthii	🌱 🌱 🌱	● ● ●			90	100+		Slimmest 'pokers'

 planting   *flowering*

99

Veronica beccabunga

Brooklime

This plant could more correctly be called the water speedwell, as it is closely related to the familiar blue-flowering wild plant. Yet the common name it most often goes by is brooklime, thought to be derived from the fact that it is frequently found growing wild in brooks on chalky ground.

It is a low, scrambling, aquatic plant that can hide a multitude of sins, such as unsightly exposed liners around the edges of ponds. The dark green, elliptic leaves are borne in profusion along branching, lighter green stems.

The dainty, royal-blue flowers appear on short, branching stalks in late spring or early summer and will fade and die off within a few weeks. The stems can reach lengths of 2m (6ft) or more, blanketing large areas.

Like watercress, brooklime can be a poor man's water clearance plant. The aerial root systems do a wonderful job of cleaning, consuming excess plant food which would otherwise encourage algae.

The genus Veronica has over 200 species, and this is not the only aquatic form; however, it is certainly the one most readily seen for sale.

Veronica beccabunga can become untidy if it is not kept trimmed. Pinching out the tips of the long stems will encourage more side growth. Fully hardy, the leaves remain until late autumn. Most growth should then be removed.

Propagate by planting up trimmings, using ordinary garden soil, and keeping them moist for a week or two. They can then be placed into the pond.

site	Performs best when grown in ponds in full sun or medium shade
temp	Very hardy, surviving temperatures as low as -20°C (-4°F)
general care	Plant during spring; remove dead stems and leaves in autumn. If allowed to, will spread indefinitely
thinning	Cut back clumps at any time of year to prevent plants taking over
pests & diseases	Mildew can sometimes be a problem but otherwise untroubled by pests and diseases

Veronica beccabunga

Zantedeschia aethiopica

Arum lily *or* Calla lily

The arum lily, originally from South Africa, is perhaps as well known as a pot plant as it is for growing in the fringes of a pond. It is sometimes referred to as the calla lily, but should not be confused with its relation *Calla palustris* (see page 85).

Zantedeschia aethiopica is quite hardy, as long as its crowns are protected in winter by a mulch of straw or bracken – or by at least 15cm (6in) of water! It is a highly variable plant, impossible to say with absolute conviction that it is hardy or half-hardy, deciduous or semi-evergreen or whether it is best as a marginal or a bog garden plant. When in full bloom, a large clump can be breathtaking.

In spring and summer, minute flowers congregate on fragrant yellow spikes, which come out from the middle of a large white spathe. The large, leathery deep green leaves, shaped like elongated hearts, are very dramatic.

The variety 'Crowborough' is taller and hardier than the species. 'Green Goddess' is particularly attractive, as spathes unfurl deep green and age to a pale, slightly ivory, emerald. 'Apple Court Babe' is a delightful miniature version, perfect for growing around a small pool or contained water

Zantedeschia aethiopica 'Crowborough'

site	Performs best when grown in ponds in full sun or partial shade
temp	Not particularly hardy, tolerating temperatures only down to -10°C (14°F)
general care	Plant Zantedeschia during spring; remove any dead stems and leaves in autumn
thinning	Lift and divide plants during spring, every three or four years
pests & diseases	Occasional fungal leaf spot, but not a serious problem. A relatively trouble-free plant

feature. The chalk white spathes are carried well above the bright green leaves.

Grow zantedeschias in full sun or partial shade, in the damp soil of a bog garden or at the edge of a pond, in water 5–30cm (2–12in) deep. Plant and divide in spring. Flowers produce many seeds, which can be sown the following autumn or spring.

Zantedeschia aethiopica

Z

Marginal Plants

	SPRING	SUMMER	AUTUMN	WINTER	height (cm)	spread (cm)	flower colour	
Zantedeschia aethiopica	🌱🌱🌱	✺✺✺			60	60	☐	Needs winter protection
Z. aethiopica 'Apple Court Babe'	🌱🌱🌱	✺✺✺			30	45	☐	Suitable for small water features
Z. aethiopica 'Crowborough'	🌱🌱🌱	✺✺✺			90	60	☐	Large flowers
Z. aethiopica 'Green Goddess'	🌱🌱🌱	✺✺✺			90	60	☐	Good for flower arranging

 planting　　 *flowering*

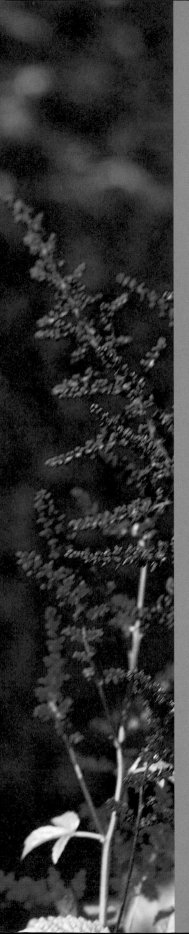

Bog Plants

Bog plants are always planted directly into the soil, and this is the main thing that distinguishes them from marginal plants, which can be grown either in the soil at the pond edge, or planted into containers that are then submerged.

A well-constructed bog garden will mimic a swampy, natural habitat. It will also, however, look beautiful, with lush foliage of different shapes, sizes and hues. A bog garden can present you with an opportunity, as well; if you have a poorly draining, soggy area of the garden, you can turn it into a beautiful bog, teeming with wildlife. The most important thing about the soil, however, is that it should be moist but not waterlogged. Nor should it ever become oxygen-deficient (anaerobic), which would create toxic, polluted conditions.

Although not water gardening in its purest form, bog gardening does have a place in this book. At one end of the bog plant list are those plant species that like to be practically in the water, and are therefore just slightly removed from the marginals. At the other end are those plants that require merely a consistently moist soil.

For plant lovers, bogs can display a vast array of seldom-seen native plants that thrive in wet or moist soil. Bog garden plants tend to dislike dry, clay soil, that resembles concrete in a hot summer, and they tend not to perform well if they are in a position exposed to high winds and the full strength of the sun all day long. Other than that, they enjoy a wide and varied selection of growing conditions.

Bogs can be part of a pond or a separate garden feature. In nature, when a bog abuts a natural pond it acts like a filter, providing an ideal mechanism for enhancing the quality of the water. Polluted water (caused by fish waste and other decomposed material) is recirculated via the bog, and as it passes through the humus-rich soil, the plants and the beneficial bacteria growing there absorb the nutrients. These plants and bacteria in turn clean the water and enhance the quality of life in the pond. Therefore if you translate this natural occurrence into a garden situation, a bog area can be incorporated into the edge of a fishpond and, in a small way, it can act as a filter. Alternatively, you can create a bog garden that is entirely separate from the pond, providing a source of water by means of a seeping hosepipe laid on the soil, or just below the surface.

Ajuga reptans
Bugle

This is a hardy, spreading plant, originally from northern Europe. It is now available in several colour forms, ranging from the dark greenish-reddish wild type, to a lighter, tricoloured cultivar.

Ajuga is a shade-loving plant that is excellent for growing under trees and shrubs – as long as the soil stays quite moist. The irony is that the leaves are not seen at their best when the plant is growing in a shady place. Yet if you transfer the plant to a sunnier spot, it sulks and never performs its best. However, it is no greater a mystery than the one surrounding its common name. No one really knows why it is called bugle.

During the winter, the leaf rosettes close up and the larger outer leaves drop away, leaving the creeping stems (stolons) with plantlets at their tips, cleary visible. Bugle is particularly suitable for growing between the paving of an informal pond surround.

The flowers are daintily attractive – short

site	Performs best when grown in bog gardens in light to medium shade
temp	Very hardy, tolerating temperatures as low as -20°C (-4°F)
general care	Plant during autumn or spring; feed in spring with a general fertilizer and water well
thinning	Trim the plant back, in autumn, if you need to restrict its spread
pests & diseases	Mildew can be a problem later in the season, but otherwise untroubled by pests and diseases

spikes of small, lipped, purple blossoms appear in spring.

Ajuga reptans 'Atropurpurea' has purple flowers, with deep purple-bronze leaves; 'Variegata' has deep green leaves with cream margins; 'Burgundy Glow' has claret coloured leaves; and 'Alba', green leaves with whitish flowers. 'Multicolor' (also known as 'Rainbow' and 'Tricolor') has blue flowers and dark bronze leaves splattered with blotches of cream, pink and red.

Looking after bugle is easy. Plant it in autumn or spring. Give it a little general fertilizer in spring and water it well during dry periods.

The best way to propagate it is by division in spring. Individual plantlets can be planted directly into the soil.

Ajuga reptans 'Burgundy Glow'

	SPRING	SUMMER	AUTUMN	WINTER	height (cm)	spread (cm)	flower colour	
Ajuga reptans					15	90	■	Plant in medium shade for best effect
A. reptans 'Alba'					15	90	□	Green leaves
A. reptans 'Atropurpurea'					15	90	■	Deep, purple-bronze leaves
A. reptans 'Burgundy Glow'					15	90	■	Claret coloured leaves
A. reptans 'Multicolor'					15	90	■	Highly variegated leaves
A. reptans 'Variegata'					15	90	■	Deep green leaves with cream margins

 planting ✹ flowering

Alchemilla
Lady's mantle

This plant has a fairly widespread origin, as it is found in the wild in light woodland habitats from Europe to Asia and even Greenland.

It is one of the most familiar of border plants, and is beloved of flower arrangers for the soft, wispy green flowers and thick uniquely serrated leaves. For the gardener it is a fine, architectural hardy herbaceous perennial.

Its suitablility for the bog garden is a matter of conjecture; for some gardeners it seems to thrive in the moist confines of a bog, whereas for others it fades rapidly, seeming to prefer a sunny, dry spot. The likely answer is the quality of the soil in the bog garden – make sure it is an open soil with plenty of humus; a waterlogged, anaerobic soil is almost certainly a deadly combination for Alchemilla.

Large, many lobed leaves with fine serrations appear to be both waxy and downy at the same time; it is a cliché to eulogize over the apparent compulsion for droplets of rainwater and dew to collect in the bowls of the leaves, but they do make this plant a little special. Tiny, soft yellow-green flowers are held in umbrella-like clusters throughout summer.

Although there are around 30 species of Lady's mantle, *Alchemilla mollis* is the form that is most often seen for sale, and is certainly the best for the bog garden.

Plant in dappled shade – direct sunlight for long periods during summer days can turn some of the leaves crispy. Mulch around the base of the plant in spring and/or autumn. It is advisable to throw a handful of general fertilizer around the base of the plant in spring. Remove the faded flowerheads and cut all old growth down to ground level at the end of autumn

Propagate by division in spring or autumn, or by seed sown in autumn. This plant will readily self-sow and come up in some unusual places in the garden; it is not, however, usually regarded as a nuisance, as the young seedlings can be most welcome.

Alchemilla mollis

site	Grows best in bog gardens in dappled shade, in moist, open soil
temp	Very hardy, tolerating temperatures to -20°C (-4°F) or lower
general care	Plant during spring; mulch plants in spring, using a light leaf mould or well-rotted garden compost
thinning	Lift and divide plants during spring, every three or four years
pests & diseases	Prone to slugs and snails, some viruses, fungal leaf spots and burrowing leaf miner grubs

	SPRING	SUMMER	AUTUMN	WINTER	height (cm)	spread (cm)	flower colour	
Alchemilla alpina	🪏 🪏 🪏	⚫ ⚫ ⚫			15	60	☐	Good ground cover plant
A. conjuncta	🪏 🪏 🪏	⚫ ⚫ ⚫			30	30	☐	Star-shaped green leaves
A. mollis	🪏 🪏 🪏	⚫ ⚫			50	50	☐	Great for flower arranging

🪏 planting   ⚫ flowering

Arum
Woodland arum

Arum italicum 'Marmoratum' (which may still be found under its old name of **Arum italicum 'Pictum'**) is a woodland plant and has three excellent qualities that makes this an ideal plant for any bog garden.

Its first quality, and providing the longest period of attraction, is the foliage, with its pretty marbling. Glossy, arrow-shaped leaves are marbled with shades of grey, yellow-green, and greenish white. Secondly, there are the flowers – greenish spathes, typical of the aroid family of plants, each with a creamy white interior. These appear in spring and are held proud of the ground.

Last but by no means least, this plant provides autumn colour with its stout spikes carrying clusters of the brightest deep-orange berries.

The straight species (*Arum italicum*), which originated in the southern parts of the UK, throughout south-east Europe and the Canary Islands, does not have the attractive leaf marbling.

A moist, but not waterlogged soil, is preferred. Plant the tubers roughly 15cm (6in) deep or, for young plants, up to the soil mark on the stem base. Little care is required once established, but it is useful if a handful of general fertilizer is applied around the base of the plant in spring.

To propagate, divide the plants – carefully, because the stem tissue is soft and easily damaged – in spring or autumn. Collect and sow seed: save the fresh, ripe fruits and wash away every trace of berry flesh; sow in a soil-based compost under glass, and be patient for germination can take several months.

site	Performs best when grown in bog gardens situated in light shade
temp	Hardy, tolerating temperatures as low as -15°C (5°F)
general care	Plant during autumn or spring; lightly feed with a general fertilizer around the base in spring
thinning	Lift and divide clumps during spring or autumn, every three or four years
pests & diseases	Slugs may eat the autumn berries, but otherwise untroubled by pests and diseases

Arum italicum

	SPRING	SUMMER	AUTUMN	WINTER	height (cm)	spread (cm)	flower colour	
Arum creticum	🌱🌼🌼🌼 🌼		🌱🌱		45	30		Attractive and unusual
A. dioscoridis	🌱🌼🌼🌼 🌼		🌱🌱		35	45		Dislikes exposed positions
A. italicum 'Marmoratum'	🌱🌼🌼🌼 🌼		🌱 🌱		55	30		Vivid autumn berries

 planting   flowering harvest

Aruncus dioicus
Goat's beard

The feathery flowerheads of goat's beard (*Aruncus dioicus*) are really most unexpected for something that is in the same plant family as the rose. The elegant leaves, majestic flowers and tall stems make this plant an erect and stately star of the bog garden. The normal species needs plenty of room in which to spread.

The mountain woods and shady streams of central Europe, China, and north America are the natural homes to this hardy perennial.

In early and mid-summer, tiny, cream-white blooms appear on large fluffy flowerheads. Arguably, Aruncus is just as attractive in the early flower stage, when the stems are delicately lined with tiny round buds, as it is when the great creamy plumes have exploded into foaming flowers.

The old name for this plant is *Aruncus sylvester*, and some nurseries may still be selling it under this name. The species is the best, but for smaller gardens there is

site	Grows best in bog gardens situated in light or moderate shade
temp	Very hardy, tolerating temperatures as low as -20°C (-4°F)
general care	Plant directly into the soil in spring or autumn; feed in the spring with a general fertilizer
thinning	Lift and divide plants during spring or autumn, every three or four years
pests & diseases	Relatively trouble free. Pests and diseases do not usually cause any problems

Aruncus dioicus

A. d. 'Kneiffii', which grows to about half the size. The leaves of this smaller form look as though they have been eaten to the veins by some creature – but this makes them very attractive in a lace-like fashion.

Plant directly into a rich, moist and leafy soil during spring or autumn. Aruncus prefers a position in light or moderate shade. There is little maintenance required: like most other perennials, cut back the dead top growth in late autumn, and take this opportunity for a general tidy-up. Mulch soil-grown plants with compost in the spring or autumn. Provide a few handfuls of general fertilizer in the spring. Aruncus has very stiff stems, so does not need staking. Clumps can grow large, so should be divided every three or four years.

Divide the spreading roots of larger clumps in spring or autumn. Or sow seeds in summer or early autumn in a humus-rich, soil-based compost and protect under glass.

	SPRING	SUMMER	AUTUMN	WINTER	height (cm)	spread (cm)	flower colour	
Aruncus dioicus	🌱 🌱 🌱	⚫ ⚫			200	120	☐	Tall, but does not need staking
A. dioicus 'Kneiffii'	🌱 🌱 🌱	⚫ ⚫			100	60	☐	Half the size of the species

🌱 planting   ⚫ flowering

Astilbe

These plants seem to appear in almost every garden – whether or not it has a bog area. They are even planted in places that are distinctly unsuited to them. However, astilbes are the most accommodating of plants. They are colourful, easy, dramatic and stately, as well as being tough and hardy.

From mid-spring onwards the deeply cut leaves appear and develop, often with purplish or bronzy green tints.

Flowering generally begins in early summer. Attractive plume-like heads of tiny flowers are followed by the rusty-brown seedheads in late summer and autumn (almost as effective as the flower spikes).

Between them, the species and hybrids provide numerous forms, from dwarf to tall, and in a multitude of shades. The hybrids borne out of *Astilbe* x *arendsii* are the most commonly seen, and these generally produce plumes up to 1m (3ft) in height. One of the best is the bright pink 'Bressingham Beauty'. 'Fire' is often found under its German name 'Feuer' and produces a brilliant red flowerhead. For possibly the purest white *arendsii* hybrid, choose 'White Queen'. The species *A. simplicifolia* has added its quota to the range of hybrids. The species is pretty, with graceful pink spikes 37cm (15in) tall, but 'Atrorosea' is superb, carrying sheaves of tiny bright pink flowers for a long time.

There is white in this range, and a charming dark-leafed, pink variety only 23cm (9in) high called 'Bronce Elegans'. For this, and the salmon 'Dunkellachs', shade as well as a humus-rich soil is needed.

'Sprite' is more adaptable. This has dark leaves and the sprays carrying masses of tiny flowers of pale shell pink make a most effective combination. It will grow to 30cm (12in), and the same across, making it ideal for the front of the border.

Astilbe x *arendsii* 'Feuer'

There are a couple of varieties from *A. japonica* that are worth mentioning. The white 'Deutschland' is regularly used for forcing as pot plants and 'Etna' carries beautiful rich red plumes above mounded foliage.

Astilbe x *arendsii* 'Venus'

site	Grows best in moist soil in light to medium shade
temp	Very hardy, surviving temperatures as low as -20°C (-4°F)
general care	Plant during spring or autumn; lightly mulch plants in spring, using a light leaf mould or well-rotted garden compost
thinning	Lift and divide plants in spring; it takes years for astilbes to get overcrowded
pests & diseases	Relatively trouble free. Pests and diseases do not usually cause any problems

'Professor van der Weilen' is a hybrid from the Japanese species *A. thunbergii*. It is a graceful plant, with handsome leaves, topped with arching sprays of creamy white flowers. It is a little taller – 1.2m (4ft) – and a little later to flower (mid- to late summer) – than most.

Where height variations are important there should be room for beauties such as *A. chinensis tacquetii* 'Superba'. This grows to 1.5m (5ft), with spikes of bright rosy purple and a long season in flower. 'Intermezzo' is mid-pink and very floriferous. Finally, there is *A. chinensis pumila*. This has a creeping habit of crispy leaves, close to the ground, and stumpy 30cm (12in) spikes of lilac rose, and is less fussy about moisture than most.

For all astilbes moisture around the roots is more important than shade – they should not be allowed to dry out. Mulch with well-rotted garden compost when the plants are dormant. Some shelter from strong winds will help, as this prolongs the flowering period.

One way to make watering more efficient is to take several large tins, such as paint pots, and pierce a few holes in them. Then sink them between the plants when the plants are dormant. Make sure that the rims are just below the soil surface. Fill the tin with water once a day during hot weather, and moisture will percolate through.

Propagate by division in spring before they start into growth; they can easily be divided when they are old and dormant.

Astilbe 'Deutschland'

	SPRING	SUMMER	AUTUMN	WINTER	height (cm)	spread (cm)	flower colour	
Astilbe 'Atrorosea'	planting	flowering	planting		37	45		Longer flowering than most
A. 'Bronce Elegans'	planting	flowering	planting		23	30		Dark-leafed
A. 'Deutschland'	planting	flowering	planting		60	45		Often grown as a pot plant
A. 'Dunkellachs'	planting	flowering	planting		23	30		Needs shade
A. 'Etna'	planting	flowering	planting		60	45		Flowers held high above the foliage
A. 'Professor Van Der Weilen'	planting	flowering	planting		120	75		Later to flower
A. 'Sprite'	planting	flowering	planting		30	30		Dark-leafed
A. chinensis 'Intermezzo'	planting	flowering	planting		100	60		Very floriferous
Astilbe chinensis pumila	planting	flowering	planting		30	60		Has a creeping habit
A. chinensis tacquetii 'Superba'	planting	flowering	planting		150	75		One of the tallest
A. simplicifolia	planting	flowering	planting		37	45		Very graceful
A. x arendsii 'Amethyst'	planting	flowering	planting		90	60		Highly popular
A. x arendsii 'Bressingham Beauty'	planting	flowering	planting		90	60		One of the oldest forms
Astilbe x arendsii 'Fanal'	planting	flowering	planting		90	60		An old but unsurpassed variety
A. x arendsii 'Federsee'	planting	flowering	planting		90	60		Has a very intense colour
A. x arendsii 'Feuer'	planting	flowering	planting		90	60		Often sold as 'Fire'
A. x arendsii 'Hyazinth'	planting	flowering	planting		90	60		Very popular form
A. x arendsii 'Irrlicht'	planting	flowering	planting		90	60		Very dark green leaves
A. x arendsii 'Snowdrift'	planting	flowering	planting		90	60		Very popular form
A. x arendsii 'Venus'	planting	flowering	planting		100	60		Slightly taller
A. x arendsii 'White Queen'	planting	flowering	planting		90	60		Possibly the most brilliant white astilbe

 planting ● flowering

Eupatorium
Hemp agrimony

Despite its common name, this is not a relative of true hemp. It is an excellent plant for attracting bees and butterflies to the bog garden, with its mass of feather-like flowers. When you look at these closely you will see that they more closely resemble daisies, as it belongs to the same plant family.

Eupatorium is not a grand or stately plant in any way, but it does show itself off well in an informal situation, and because of its propensity for attracting wildlife, it is worth making room for. Coarse, oval leaves are arranged along the full length of the tall stems. The flowers, which are carried from late summer to mid-autumn, are cream-white. In the case of *Eupatorium purpureum* subsp. *maculatum*, commonly referred to as Joe Pye weed, the flowers are rose-purple.

Mulch in spring and autumn and apply a balanced fertilizer to the soil around the plant annually in early spring. In late autumn, after the foliage has started to die back, cut any remaining growth right down to soil level.

Eupatorium cannabinum 'Chocolate'

site	Grows best in bog gardens situated in full sun or light shade
temp	Very hardy, tolerating temperatures as low as -20°C (-4°F)
general care	Plant during spring; lightly mulch plants in spring, using leaf mould or well-rotted garden compost
thinning	Lift and divide plants during spring, every two or three years
pests & diseases	Relatively trouble free. Pests and diseases do not usually cause any problems

The best method of propagation is by sowing seed in the autumn, using a moist soil-based compost. Keep the young plants in an unheated greenhouse or coldframe for protection while they are still shooting through. When the plants are large enough to handle, prick them out; they should be ready for planting out in spring. Alternatively, mature plants can also be divided in spring.

	SPRING	SUMMER	AUTUMN	WINTER	height (cm)	spread (cm)	flower colour	
Eupatorium cannabinum	🌱		● ●	● ●	150	60		Feather-like flowers
E. cannabinum 'Chocolate'	🌱	● ● ●	● ●	● ●	150	60		Double flowers
E. purpureum subsp. *maculatum*	🌱	● ● ●	● ●	● ●	200	60		Magnificent, structural plant

 planting   flowering

Filipendula
Meadowsweet

The most frequently seen form of meadowsweet is the European _Filipendula ulmaria_, which is ideal for all but the smallest of bog gardens. It is a tall, moisture-loving, bushy plant that works well around the edge of a pond or as a transition to the rest of the garden. Sometimes called Queen-of-the-Meadow, it is a hardy pink or white flowering perennial. The blooms are tiny, and the flowerheads feathery.

For the smaller garden choose _Filipendula ulmaria_ 'Aurea', a white-flowered cultivar that grows only 30cm (12in) or so in height. It needs half shade to preserve the beautiful yellow colouring of the leaves.

F. ulmaria 'Variegata' gets its name from the plant's leaves, which are dark green with lemon yellow centres. Creamy white flowers bloom on branching stems in high summer. 'Flore Pleno' produces unusual white flowers that are double.

F. rubra 'Venusta' needs plenty of room, but is a superb plant in the right place. Dark green leaves are overtopped by large feathery deep rose pink flowers on tall stems.

Mulch in spring and autumn, and apply a general fertilizer to the root area in spring. The stems are tough and sturdy, so will not need staking. Cut down dead foliage and stems in autumn.

To propagate, sow fresh seed in autumn or divide plants in spring or autumn.

Filipendula rubra 'Venusta'

site	Performs best when situated in bog gardens in light shade
temp	Very hardy, tolerating temperatures as low as -20°C (-4°F)
general care	Plant during spring; lightly mulch plants in spring, using leaf mould or well-rotted garden compost
thinning	Lift and divide plants during spring, every three or four years
pests & diseases	Aphids may infest plants, but will not do any lasting damage. Otherwise, relatively trouble free

	SPRING	SUMMER	AUTUMN	WINTER	height (cm)	spread (cm)	flower colour	
Filipendula rubra 'Venusta'	🌱🌱🌱	● ●			200	90	▨	The tallest meadowsweet
F. ulmaria	🌱🌱🌱	● ●			90	60	☐	Good for attracting insects
F. ulmaria 'Aurea'	🌱🌱🌱	● ●			30	20	☐	Golden leaves
F. ulmaria 'Flore Pleno'	🌱🌱🌱	● ● ●			75	45	☐	Unusual double flowers
F. ulmaria 'Variegata'	🌱🌱🌱	● ●			90	60	☐	Green and yellow leaves

🌱 planting　　● flowering

Gentiana
Gentian

Gentiana pneumonanthe is a moisture-loving member of this genus which produces clusters of rich, deep blue trumpet-shaped flowers. They appear at the ends of the stems during mid- to late summer. No other bog garden plant will provide as intense a blue as this unusual but very choice wild flower.

Gentiana pneumonanthe (Marsh gentian) is a dramatic blue gentian found wild right across the Northern Hemisphere. The flowers are large and trumpet-shaped, sometimes also resembling bells or urns. The leaves are lush green, shiny and lance-shaped on short, slender stems. For this plant to thrive and achieve its full impact, the soil needs to be damp and rich in organic matter and, perhaps most important of all, acid.

A position in full sun or light to moderate shade is required. The best time to plant is during spring. Straight after planting, mulch with garden compost, and do this annually each spring, along with a feed of general fertilizer. If the leaves turn

site	Performs best when grown in bog gardens in full sun or light shade
temp	Very hardy, tolerating temperatures as low as -20°C (-4°F)
general care	Plant during spring; feed with a general fertilizer and mulch plants annually in spring
thinning	Lift and divide plants during spring only when they get old; resent being disturbed
pests & diseases	Prone to slugs and snails, some viruses, fungal leaf spots and burrowing leaf miner grubs

Gentiana pneumonanthe

yellow in summer, the soil is not acid enough, so water it with sequestered iron to restore the pH levels. This gentian resents disturbance, so leave it well alone once it is established. Like other late-flowering gentians, *Gentiana pneumonanthe* associates well with small, late-flowering bulbs, as well as ferns and grasses.

The willow gentian (*G. asclepiadea*) produces typical gentian-blue flowers on stems up to 60cm (24in) high, and tolerates some lime in the soil; it also has a white form, *G. asclepiadea* var. *alba*, and various pink or pale blue varieties.

To increase stock of both forms of Gentian, take softwood cuttings in summer, rooting them in a propagator with slight bottom heat. Seeds can be sown in early spring, again in a propagator, and kept at around 20°C (68°F).

	SPRING	SUMMER	AUTUMN	WINTER	height (cm)	spread (cm)	flower colour	
Gentiana asclepiadea					90	60		Arching stems
G. asclepiadea var. *alba*					90	60		Dramatic plant
G. pneumonanthe					30	25		Bog plant with the most intense blue flowers

 planting   flowering

Geum rivale
Water avens

This is a hardy woodland plant, which enjoys a wetter soil than most of the garden geums. It is vastly under rated. Its compact, deeply lobed green leaves are soft to the touch, eventually forming dense clumps that, in the wild, slowly colonize river banks.

It is closely related to the garden geums, but its flowers are much daintier. They are small, bell-like, pinkish purple, and hang in loose heads on arching, hairy stalks that nod and sway in the breeze. They appear during late spring and early summer, and are followed by furry, mace-like seed heads that are equally attractive in their own right.

The leaves are small, rich green, rounded and slightly toothed at the edges.

There are several selected forms and hybrids of *Geum rivale*, but these can be difficult to find in garden centres. They include 'Coppertone': which has brown flower stems and slightly pendent flowers; 'Lemon Drops' with yellowish flowers; 'Leonard's Variety', with coppery-pink flowers; and 'Lionel Cox', which has creamy white flowers. Although these are all attractive varieties, they have not been included in the table below as they are not always commonly available.

Geum rivale

site	Grows best in bog gardens situated in full sun or light shade
temp	Very hardy, tolerating temperatures as low as -20°C (-4°F)
general care	Plant during autumn/spring; lightly mulch plants in autumn with leaf mould or well-rotted garden compost
thinning	Lift and divide plants during spring, every three or four years
pests & diseases	Can be prone to attack by sawflies and leaf miners, but otherwise relatively trouble free

It is quite an easy plant to care for. Plant out in spring or autumn in a lightly shaded spot. If planting more than one, set them out 30cm (12in) apart. These plants are more or less self-sufficient. They do not require staking. To get the optimum in growth and flowering, mulch around the root areas in autumn using moist, well-rotted garden compost. A little extra food, in the form of bone meal should be applied in early spring. Cut down old foliage in late autumn.

To propagate, divide the plants in autumn or spring; after three or four years they will need to be split anyway. Alternatively, during late spring sow seed straight into pots of damp soil, covering lightly, and place in a warm, shady spot.

	SPRING	SUMMER	AUTUMN	WINTER	height (cm)	spread (cm)	flower colour	
Geum rivale					45	18		Roots can be in water permanently
G. rivale 'Album'					15	20		Shorter growing
G. rivale 'Cream Drop'					15	20		Modern cultivar

planting   flowering

Gunnera

The genus Gunnera contains some plants that are on the tender side: while the large *Gunnera manicata* merely needs some winter protection, the creeping *G. magellanica* should be brought under cover for winter.

The most familiar gunnera is *Gunnera manicata* and it is almost compulsory for those with big water gardens to grow it. It is the largest of any hardy herbaceous plant, and many call it the giant or prickly rhubarb, because of the similarity of its leaves; in truth the two plants are not even related. Close inspection will show that the plants are very different, Gunnera being more spectacular. As long as there is sufficient space, even in a small garden, gunnera will help to create an exotic atmosphere. The oversized leaves afford shelter for all manner of garden wildlife, even waterfowl.

The vast jagged and indented leaves are the main reason for growing this plant.

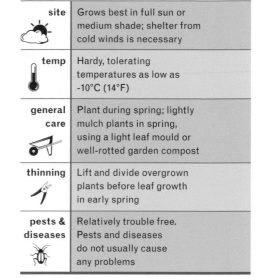

site	Grows best in full sun or medium shade; shelter from cold winds is necessary
temp	Hardy, tolerating temperatures as low as -10°C (14°F)
general care	Plant during spring; lightly mulch plants in spring, using a light leaf mould or well-rotted garden compost
thinning	Lift and divide overgrown plants before leaf growth in early spring
pests & diseases	Relatively trouble free. Pests and diseases do not usually cause any problems

Individual leaves on some mature plants can reach to 2m (6ft) in diameter. They are carried on thick stems with nasty spikes on the largest.

Conical clusters of small, greenish-brown flowers appear in late spring and early summer. The flower spikes can reach 1.5m (5ft) in height. Rust-brown seed pods follow.

The giant Chilean rhubarb (*G. tinctoria*) is slightly smaller and slightly hardier. Leaves on mature plants are 1m (3ft) wide and the overall height is 2m (7ft). Alternatively, you could opt for the dwarf, carpet-creeping gunnera, *G. magellanica*. It has bright green 'crinkled' leaves and plants barely reach 10cm (4in) in height, with a spread of just 1m (3ft).

Choose a position in full sun or medium shade, at the edge of larger ponds. Gunneras are tolerant of most soils, but prefer deep, fertile soils with high moisture content. Plant during spring. Feed with a general fertilizer in spring. They are undemanding plants, as long as they have some shelter from the coldest of winds and the latest of frosts. Cut back the dry leaves in autumn. In colder areas, give the plants a protective mulch with straw or sacking; some gardeners use the old leaves to cover the plants.

Propagate by division of larger clumps in spring, or by seeds sown fresh in the autumn. Choose a loam-based compost and store the growing seed in a sheltered cold frame.

Gunnera manicata

		SPRING	SUMMER	AUTUMN	WINTER	height (cm)	spread (cm)	flower colour	
Gunnera magellanica						10	100		Small, crinkly edged leaves
G. manicata						300	500		Leaves 2m (6ft) across
G. tinctoria						200	300		Leaves 1m (3ft) across

 planting ☀ flowering

Hemerocallis
Daylily

Daylilies are so called because each individual flower does last only a day. Plants can be grown in any part of the garden, but they perform best in reasonably moist soil, which means that they can make luxuriant additions to any bog garden. The appeal of these plants is added to by the fact that they are so easy to grow and propagate.

Hemerocallis has come in for a great deal of attention over the past century from hybridists in Europe and North America. A few keen growers in the early 1900s raised many beautiful varieties. This encouraged dozens of other hybridists to 'have a go', and several thousand named forms have since been created. Many have disappeared from cultivation because they were surpassed in excellence by newer forms. Even so, there are well over 300 varieties available to the gardener today (and many more still in the USA, where certain sections of the gardening community regard them as cult plants).

The individual trumpet-shaped flowers are not particularly attractive in their own right, particularly when they are a day old and are on the wane. The real beauty is when you see a mass of flowers. The varieties that produce flowers of a single colour are more attractive than those that

Hemerocallis 'Pink Charm'

have their main colour concentrated inside the trumpet, where it can only be seen if the flower is looked at end on. Also, nearly all the yellow varieties are scented, whereas most of the others are lacking this attribute.

The single coloured flowers, where the colour is repeated on the outside of the trumpet, give a much more effective impression and make a more impressive statement in a border. But beware of some of the 'red' varieties (there is no true scarlet or carmine yet available): they can look very scrappy en masse and add nothing positive to the overall effect of the border.

The rushy leaves are a feature in their own right in spring: the brightest of greens, arching and growing almost 3cm (1in) a day. At flowering time the leaves are fully complementary to the trumpet flowers, which are produced on smooth stems.

Although there are several species available, these tend to be found only in specialists' gardens or nurseries. The earliest to show colour, in late spring, is the dwarf species *Hemerocallis dumortierii*, which has yellow flowers lasting for several weeks. *H. citrina* and *H. lilioasphodelus* are charming, fragrant

Hemerocallis 'Black Magic'

yellow species for late spring and early summer. Another species of note, *H. multiflora*, produces pale orange-yellow flowers in great profusion from mid-summer to mid-autumn.

The following is a list of some of the best garden hybrids. *H.* 'Orangeman', first bred in 1906, has deep orange coloured flowers. *H.* 'Hyperion' was introduced over 50 years ago, and is still in demand for its clear colour and large yellow flowers; a newer and outstanding yellow colour is the hybrid *H.* 'Lark Song'. Then there is *H.* 'Black Magic', with its deep ruby mahogany flowers; *H.* 'Contessa', which

Hemerocallis 'Pink Damask'

site	Performs best when situated in full sun or light shade
temp	Very hardy, tolerating temperatures as low as -20°C (-4°F)
general care	Plant during spring or autumn; mulch plants in spring, using well-rotted garden compost
thinning	Lift and divide plants during spring, every three or four years
pests & diseases	Relatively trouble free. Pests and diseases do not usually cause any problems

produces light orange blooms; *H.* 'Bonanza', with its soft yellow colour but a dwarf hybrid, matching well with the deeper coloured *H.* 'Golden Chimes', which is also dwarf.

H. 'Dubloon' (sometimes sold as 'Golden Orchid') produces rich golden coloured flowers. The old variety *H.* 'Pink Damask' still holds its own as one of the closest daylilies to true pink. Other excellent forms include *H.* 'Little Wine Cup', which has burgundy red blooms with a yellow throat; *H.* 'Cream Drop', with its small, creamy yellow flowers; *H.* 'Buzz Bomb', which is a deep, velvety red, and *H.* 'Chartreuse Magic', which produces canary yellow and green flowers.

There are only a handful of double-flowered varieties, and they do not generally add much to the range. Arguably the best double Hemerocallis is *H. fulva* 'Flore Pleno', with its reddish orange coloured flowers.

Daylilies can be planted at any time from mid-autumn until mid-spring. The soil should be

Hemerocallis 'Crimson Pirate'

Hemerocallis 'Buzz Bomb'

enriched in advance, and when fully established some general fertilizer and mulching in spring will help in the production of fine flowers.

The preferred site for most Hemerocallis would be to plant them in full sun or light shade (heavy shade can often depress flower production). Most soils are tolerated, but these plants perform best in fairly rich, loamy soil.

Maintenance is fairly easy. Cut back any dead flowerstalks to the base, as soon as the last flowers on them have faded. Cut away all foliage, right back to soil level, in the autumn. If you leave this, then the foliage will simply turn to an untidy mess over winter.

For propagation, lift and divide overgrown plants in autumn or spring. Alternatively, sow seed in containers in a cold frame or greenhouse in autumn or spring.

	SPRING	SUMMER	AUTUMN	WINTER	height (cm)	spread (cm)	flower colour	
Hemerocallis 'Black Magic'	planting	flowering	planting		90	90	■	Looks good next to 'Cream Drop'
H. 'Bonanza'	planting	flowering	planting		60	60	□	Dwarf cultivar
H. 'Buzz Bomb'	planting	flowering	planting		90	90	■	One of the deepest coloured forms
H. 'Chartreuse Magic'	planting	flowering	planting		90	90	□	Unusual flower colour
H. citrina	planting	flowering	planting		75	75	□	Early flowering
H. 'Contessa'	planting	flowering	planting		90	90	■	Modern, outstanding variety
H. 'Crimson Pirate'	planting	flowering	planting		90	90	■	Modern, popular variety
H. 'Dubloon'	planting	flowering	planting		90	90	■	Sometimes sold as 'Golden Orchid'
H. dumortierii	planting, flowering	flowering	planting		45	60	■	One of the earliest to flower
H. fulva 'Flore Pleno'	planting	flowering	planting		120	90	□	Double flowers
H. 'Golden Chimes'	planting	flowering	planting		75	60	□	Dwarf cultivar
H. 'Hyperion'	planting	flowering	planting		90	90	□	Large flowers
H. 'Lark Song'	planting	flowering	planting		90	90	□	Modern, outstanding variety
H. lilioasphodelus	planting	flowering	planting		60	60	■	Early and fragrant
H. 'Little Wine Cup'	planting	flowering	planting		90	90	■	Each flower has a yellow 'throat'
H. multiflora	planting	flowering	flowering		90	90	■	Flowers into mid-autumn
H. 'Orangeman'	planting	flowering	planting		90	90	■	Old variety – bred in 1906
H. 'Pink Charm'	planting	flowering	planting		90	90	□	Modern, popular variety

planting　　flowering

Hosta
Plantain lily

Hostas are, of course, principally grown for their large, graceful leaves. First introduced to our gardens in the late 1700s, with the Chinese _Hosta plantaginea_, others quickly followed, mainly from Japan. There are more than 70 species and hundreds of modern varieties (which are being added to every year, particularly from plant breeders in the USA).

There are few hardy herbaceous plants that can match the variety, diversity of form, texture and leaf colourings as the hosta. These are fast-spreading, clump-forming plants that enhance any waterside environment.

They have always been thought of as plants for the damp, shadier parts of the garden, but most gardeners now recognise them as much more versatile plants, often tolerating sunny, dry spots too.

The leaves vary in size from those which are just a few centimetres (couple of inches) long, to the largest which are dinner plate-sized. Just as the sizes vary,

site	Grows best in light shade, although they sometimes do well in full sun
temp	Very hardy, surviving temperatures as low as -20°C (-4°F)
general care	Plant during spring or autumn; lightly mulch plants in spring, using well-rotted garden compost
thinning	Lift and divide plants during the spring, every three or four years
pests & diseases	Slugs and snails are the main problem, but otherwise hostas are untroubled by pests and diseases

Best known as foliage plants, hostas also produce attractive flower spikes

so too do the textures of the leaves, from very smooth, through to shiny, dull, matt and even corrugated. Add to these variables the bewildering array of leaf colours and variegations, and one can see why they are among some of our most popular plants.

In summer they produce long stems of small, nodding, lily-like flowers in shades of lilac, mauve and purple, as well as a few which are pure white. Some selections are even fragrant.

Probably the most popular species of hosta is _Hosta fortunei_, and one of the most attractive forms is _H. fortunei_ var. _albopicta_. It has bright yellow leaves distinctively edged with green in spring, which change to all-over green as they age. Meanwhile, _H. fortunei_ var. _aureomarginata_ (syn. _H._ 'Fortunei Aureomarginata') has leaves of a rich dark green with a yellow border, and _H. fortunei_ var. _hyacinthina_ has slightly shiny, small green leaves with long points.

H. crispula is a great favourite, with striking white-margined broad, pointed dark green leaves. It also offers stems of lilac-purple flowers in mid-summer. *H. decorata* has bold ribbed leaves with cream margins; it also produces pale purple flowers. *H. elata* is among the earliest of hostas to flower, producing pale lilac blooms in the early summer, held aloft pale green matt leaves with wavy edges.

Wavy edged foliage is a characteristic of the varieties of *H. undulata*. One of the earliest varieties is *H. undulata* var. *albomarginata* (also seen sometimes named 'Thomas Hogg'); it has a strong

Hosta sieboldiana

H. fortunei var. aureomarginata

Hosta fortunei

creamy-white edge to the leaves.

There are several hundred cultivars and hybrid hostas from which to choose, and if you wanted to start a small collection (for they can be addictive plants) you would be well advised to consult one of the growing number of nurseries specializing in them.

Plant hostas in spring, preferably in a place that receives full sun or dappled shade at the most. Mulch in spring or autumn, and give a handful of general fertilizer for each plant in spring. Cut back any dead flower stalks as soon as they have faded, and cut or pull away tattered foliage as soon as it starts to look bad.

Division of hosta clumps during the autumn or spring is the best way to propagate this plant. If you delay carrying out this until the new growths have started to appear in spring, it is possible to prise the clumps away from the main crown of the plant without having to lift the complete thing.

The biggest problem any gardener is

likely to have with growing hostas is the damage caused by slugs and snails, which find the leaves delectable. Frequent 'baiting' around the plants with proprietary poison-based pellets, gels or tapes is commonplace.

Gardeners who prefer the organic approach to tackle these predators often use half grapefruits or small sunken cups containing beer. Both will attract the pests,

at which point you can gather them up and dispose of them in the way that suits you. This should be carried out from mid-spring onwards. Failure to do this will result in badly chewed leaves which can soon become an eyesore. Moreover, it will ruin the elegant display which a tightly planted group of different hosta varieties or species can offer.

Hosta undulata var. univittata

	SPRING		SUMMER		AUTUMN		WINTER		height (cm)	spread (cm)	flower colour	
Hosta 'August Moon'	🌱 🌱	✹	✹ ✹		🌱 🌱			75	50		Pale green to soft yellow
H. 'Big Daddy'	🌱 🌱	✹	✹ ✹		🌱 🌱			90	100		Glaucous blue leaves
H. 'Blue Angel'	🌱 🌱	✹	✹ ✹		🌱 🌱			120	100		Blue-grey
H. 'Bressingham Blue'	🌱 🌱	✹	✹ ✹		🌱 🌱			90	150		Glaucous blue leaves
H. crispula	🌱 🌱	✹	✹		🌱 🌱			45	90		Deep green leave with a wide white margin
H. decorata	🌱 🌱	✹	✹ ✹		🌱 🌱			30	45		Dark green leaves with white margins
H. elata	🌱 🌱	✹	✹ ✹		🌱 🌱			65	100		Mid-green leaves with large, sunken veins
H. fortunei	🌱 🌱	✹	✹ ✹		🌱 🌱			75	90		Heart-shaped mid-green leaves
H. fortunei var. aureomarginata	🌱 🌱		✹ ✹		🌱 🌱			75	90		Green leaves with cream-yellow edges
H. fortunei var. hyacinthina	🌱 🌱		✹ ✹		🌱 🌱			75	90		Silvery grey to blue-green leaves
H. 'Gold Edger'	🌱 🌱		✹ ✹		🌱 🌱			30	70		Soft yellow leaves
H. 'Hadspen Blue'	🌱 🌱		✹ ✹		🌱 🌱			30	30		Deep glaucous blue leaves
H. sieboldiana	🌱 🌱	✹	✹		🌱 🌱			90	150		Leaves turn dull green in full sun
H. undulata var. univittata	🌱 🌱		✹ ✹		🌱 🌱			40	70		Very good in shade and under trees
H. ventricosa	🌱 🌱			✹ ✹	🌱 🌱			70	90		Dark green wavy-edged leaves

🌱 planting   ✹ flowering

Iris

Bog garden iris

On pages 66–70 we considered the irises that like to sit with their roots in water. There are also a number of species that flourish in the damp soil of a bog garden; only two species are really popular and neither of them likes over-wet soil in winter.

On pages 66–70

The Siberian iris, *Iris sibirica*, is vastly underrated, but few sights can surpass a massed planting of them during late spring when they are in full flower. Colours available are white, through all shades of blue to deepest purple. Forming large clumps of grassy leaves, they are extremely easy to grow and problem free. They will grow quite happily in any kind of soil. After four years or so, the centres of clumps tend to become 'bald' with a ring of growth progressively moving outwards each year, and it is at this stage that the plant should be divided.

At flowering time the first of two buds from each stem opens; the second bud opens as the first fades. At the end of the flowering season the highly glossy green seed pods are formed, and these have an attraction all of their own; remove them if you want to preserve the plant's energy for better flowering the following year.

I. sibirica flowers are smaller than most water irises, but there are many varieties and several good dwarf forms, including 'Flight of Butterflies' (dark blue veined purple) and 'Perry's Pygmy' (dark blue).

I. ensata (still sometimes sold as *I. kaempferi*) is the delightful Japanese clematis iris, so called because the blooms flatten out to resemble the star-shaped blooms of

site	Performs best grown in bog gardens in full sun, but will tolerate light shade	
temp	Hardy, surviving temperatures down to -15°C (5°F)	
general care	Plant during spring and autumn; lightly mulch plants in spring, using well-rotted garden compost	
thinning	Lift and divide overcrowded plants at any time during the spring	
pests & diseases	Snails can inflict some damage to these plants and aphids can infest the young flower buds	

Iris sibirica

Bog Plants

clematis. Provided it has been given a sunny position, plenty of moisture in the growing season and a rich soil, it is undemanding. Although it prefers an acid soil, it can be grown in chalky or limestone soil, but may not be as tall in these conditions. It grows to a height of between 60–75cm (24–30in), and flowers during late spring and early summer.

The leaves are broad and the flowers are large and flattened. From the elegant three-petalled single blooms to the huge six-petalled doubles that can reach 30cm (12in) across, they are breathtaking in their colour range and beauty.

Some of the best singles include: 'Apollo' (white with yellow); 'Darling' (lavender pink with darker veins); 'Rose Queen' (deep sugar pink), and 'Variegata' (deep purple flowers with grey-green and white striped leaves).

Of the double forms, look for: 'Blue Peter' (deep blue and yellow); 'Dresden China' (pale pink ageing to translucent white); 'Mandarin' (purple and yellow), and 'Oku-Banri' (white edged petunia pink).

If the ground remains very wet in winter, try growing the less popular *I. orientalis*, formerly known as *I. ochroleuca*. It usually grows to 90cm (3ft) and produces white and egg-yolk yellow flowers.

To vegetatively propagate all of these irises, especially if the desire is to keep the offspring true to their parent, dividing the clumps after flowering is the only method. In most cases, the sooner this is done after the flowers fade, the better, but with *I. ensata* it is best to wait until autumn, before the leaves have finally died down. *I. ensata* can be grown from seed.

Iris ensata 'Reveil'

	SPRING	SUMMER	AUTUMN	WINTER	height (cm)	spread (cm)	flower colour	
Iris ensata 'Apollo'					90	30		Single flowers
I. ensata 'Blue Peter'					90	30		Double flowers
I. ensata 'Darling'					60	30		Single flowers
I. ensata 'Dresden China'					90	30		Double flowers
I. ensata 'Mandarin'					110	30		Large double flowers
I. ensata 'Oku-Banri'					90	30		Double flowers
I. ensata 'Reveil'					75	30		Single flowers
I. ensata 'Variegata'					90	30		Grey-green and white striped leaves
I. orientalis					90	30		Likes very wet soil
I. sibirica					90	30		Natural species
I. sibirica 'Alba'					60	30		Slightly later flowering
I. sibirica 'Caezar'					75	30		Earlier flowering
I. sibirica 'Emperor'					120	30		One of the tallest forms
I. sibirica 'Flight of Butterflies'					90	30		Popular modern hybrid
I. sibirica 'Helen Astor'					60	30		A good colour variant
I. sibirica 'Ottawa'					60	30		Popular modern hyrbid
I. sibirica 'Perry's Blue'					90	30		Most frequently seen form
I. sibirica 'Perry's Pygmy'					60	30		Dwarf form

  planting   flowering

Leucojum
Snowflake

There are few plants that grow from bulbs which are suitable for the bog garden, but this is one of them. Easily confused with a snowdrop, *Leucojum vernum*, the spring snowflake, is a larger plant, flowering with dainty bells from late winter to mid-spring. The blooms are white, with green or yellow spots, bell-shaped and nodding. Leaves are strap-like, rich green and grow in tufts.

Leucojum aestivum is the summer snowflake. It is taller than its spring cousin, at 60cm (2ft), and the early summer flowers are slightly larger. Arguably the best form is 'Gravetye Giant'. Avoid growing the autumn snowflake (*L. autumnale*) in the bog garden, as it prefers drier conditions.

Plant from early to mid-autumn, setting the bulbs 7.5cm (3in) or so deep and 10cm (4in) apart. Plant in groups of five or more for best effect.

Mulch over the bulb area in autumn and give the plants a general fertilizer in spring. Remove the faded blooms and divide overcrowded clumps after four or five years.

To propagate, sow bulbs in late summer in a cold frame. Alternatively, divide the clumps after flowering and before the leaves die down.

Leucojum vernum

Leucojum aestivum

site	Grows best in bog gardens situated in full sun or light shade
temp	Hardy, tolerating temperatures down to around -15°C (5°F)
general care	Plant blubs during autumn; lightly mulch around plants in autumn; apply a general fertiliser in spring
thinning	Lift and divide overgrown clumps during spring, every four or five years
pests & diseases	Relatively trouble free. Pests and diseases do not usually cause any problems

	SPRING	SUMMER	AUTUMN	WINTER	height (cm)	spread (cm)	flower colour	
Leucojum aestivum	🌱	⚫ ⚫	🌱 🌱		60	20	☐	Tallest form
L. aestivum 'Gravetye Giant'	🌱	⚫ ⚫	🌱 🌱		60	20	☐	Larger flowers
L. vernum	⚫		🌱 🌱 🌱	⚫	20	10	☐	Early flowering

🌱 planting   ⚫ flowering

Lychnis
Ragged robin

An attractive flower of natural marshes and damp places, Lychnis is not one of the more spectacular of bog plants, yet it is always welcome – and lovely in a wild waterside context.

Large, pink-fringed blooms are carried on long, reddish stalks, from late spring to mid-summer. The leaves are narrow and sparse, and grow in thin clumps.

The white-flowered *Lychnis flos-cuculi* var. *albiflora* is worth making room for, as is the dwarf pink form 'Nana'.

The best related plant for a bog garden is *L. chalcedonica* (also known as the Maltese cross, the Jerusalem cross or catchfly). It does catch one or two aphids on its felt-like leaves, but not enough to warrant it being used as a biological control for these pests! The flowers are flame-red in early summer on 1m (3ft) high stems. A white variety, (*L. chalcedonica* var. *albiflora*) and a double-flowered form 'Flore Pleno' are often seen.

The best garden position for these is in full sun or light shade, in any moist (or even wet) soil. Plant in autumn or spring, spacing them some 15cm (6in) apart, in small groups. Cut down all growth in autumn, but otherwise they are relatively undemanding plants.

To propagate, sow fresh seeds in a cold frame in spring. Alternatively, divide clumps in autumn or spring.

site	Grows best in bog gardens situated in full sun or light shade
temp	Fairly hardy, tolerating temperatures as low as -20°C (-4°F)
general care	Plant during spring; cut down all growth in autumn. Lightly mulch and give plants a feed in spring
thinning	Lift and divide plants during spring, every three or four years
pests & diseases	Relatively trouble free. Pests and diseases do not usually cause any problems

Lychnis chalcedonica

Bog Plants

L

	SPRING	SUMMER	AUTUMN	WINTER	height (cm)	spread (cm)	flower colour	
Lychnis chalcedonica	planting	flowering			90	30	■	Catches flies on its felty leaves
L. chalcedonica var. albiflora	planting	flowering			90	30	□	Stands out with its bright flowers
L. chalcedonica 'Flore Pleno'	planting	flowering			90	30	■	Double flowers
L. flos-cuculi	planting	flowering			60	30	▨	Reddish flower stalks
L. flos-cuculi var. albiflora	planting	flowering			60	30	□	Typical cottage garden flower
L. flos-cuculi 'Nana'	planting	flowering			45	30	▨	Dwarf form

 planting   flowering

Lysichiton
Skunk cabbage

Lysichiton has an unpleasant common name – sniff the foliage at close quarters, and you will see from the heavy aroma why it is so called! It is, however, a wonderful plant and a real star of the bog garden. It is also referred to as the American bog arum, and the botanical name is often spelt wrongly as *Lysichitum americanum*.

Lysichiton's eye-catching golden yellow spathe flowers, in typical arum style, appear in mid-spring before the foliage. Each spathe can be 30cm (12in) in length. It really pays to grow this next to water, where the reflection can add to the magnificence. The leaves, which appear in late spring, are long, rounded and a fresh yellow-green. The oriental bog arum (*Lysichiton camtschatcensis*) is a slightly smaller plant, with creamy white spathes.

Plant from mid-autumn to early spring, 75cm (30in) apart. Plants may prove a little slow to flower, but they are well worth persevering with. The soil should be enriched with plenty of organic matter. The best position is in partial shade, although it likes growing in full sun almost as much. This is an undemanding plant, but it would pay to provide twice-yearly mulches in spring and autumn. Feed with a general fertilizer in spring. Do not disturb the plants once they are established.

To propagate, sow fresh seed in moist soil during late spring or early summer. Self-sown seedlings can be transplanted at any time. Or remove young offsets, taking as much root as you can gather, so as not to disturb the whole plant.

site	Grows best in partial shade, although full sun does not harm it
temp	Hardy, tolerating temperatures down to -15°C (5°F)
general care	Plant from mid-autumn to early spring; mulch in spring and autumn with well-rotted garden compost or manure
thinning	Lift and divide plants during spring, every three or four years
pests & diseases	Relatively trouble free. Pests and diseases do not usually cause any problems

Lysichiton americanus

	SPRING	SUMMER	AUTUMN	WINTER	height (cm)	spread (cm)	flower colour	
Lysichiton americanus	🌱 🌼🌼		🌱 🌱	🌱 🌱 🌱	90	60	⬜	Leaves are pungent at close quarters
L. camtschatcensis	🌱 🌼🌼		🌱 🌱	🌱 🌱 🌱	75	60	◻	Slightly smaller

🌱	planting	✹	flowering

Lythrum

Purple
loosestrife

This is an impressive plant, especially when a large group is in full bloom. In the wild type, *L. salicaria* (the form that is best for wildlife ponds), the tall flower spikes are purple-pink and can attain a height of 2m (6ft) or more. One feature that makes this plant so attractive as a wildlife waterside plant is that it attracts bees, several types of butterflies and other insects.

The various garden cultivars tend to be shorter than the wild form, and with lighter coloured flowers. All have attractive autumn colouring.

Lythrum is an adaptable plant that will grow in anything from dry soil, to a position where its roots are permanently in water. To obtain the best results, however, plant it in a good, moist situation in full sun. Self-sown seedlings can be difficult to weed out, so cut off the flowerheads if you do not want the plants to spread.

The two species that offer the best potential for bog gardens are *Lythrum salicaria* and *L. virgatum*. The former is the natural loosestrife found in the wild and a

Lythrum salicaria

number of excellent hybrids have been bred from it. *L. virgatum* is, arguably, more suitable for the small bog garden, as its hybrids are slightly shorter in height and the flower spikes are generally more dainty.

To propagate, divide clumps during autumn or transplant self-sown seedlings in spring (note that these seedlings do not always produce the same flower colours as the parent plants).

site	Grows best in bog gardens situated in full sun or light shade
temp	Very hardy, surviving temperatures as low as -20°C (-4°F)
general care	Plant during spring; lightly mulch plants in spring, using a light leaf mould or well-rotted garden compost
thinning	Lift and divide plants during spring, every three or four years
pests & diseases	Relatively trouble free. Pests and diseases do not usually cause any problems

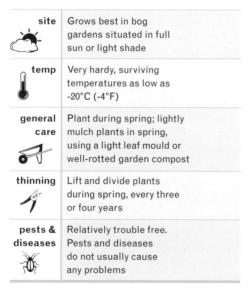

	SPRING	SUMMER	AUTUMN	WINTER	height (cm)	spread (cm)	flower colour	
Lythrum salicaria	🌱🌱🌱	⚫⚫⚫			200	30	■	Good for attracting insects
L. salicaria 'Firecandle'	🌱🌱🌱	⚫⚫⚫			120	30	■	Often sold as 'Feuerkerze'
L. salicaria 'Robert'	🌱🌱🌱	⚫⚫⚫			90	30	■	Garden form most likely to be found
L. salicaria 'The Beacon'	🌱🌱🌱	⚫⚫⚫			120	30	■	Intense flower colour
L. virgatum 'Rosy Gem'	🌱🌱🌱	⚫⚫⚫			90	30	■	Excellent modern hybrid
L. virgatum 'The Rocket'	🌱🌱🌱	⚫⚫⚫			90	30	■	Very dainty flower spikes

 planting   flowering

Phormium tenax

New Zealand flax

This plant makes a valuable addition to the bog garden for the simple fact that it is the only sword-leaved plant that really enjoys a permanently moist soil. It is often grown as a dry border plant, where its qualities as an architectural plant are well known.

Most phormiums are large, clump-forming plants, with the bonus of keeping their leaves all year round. The best forms have variegated foliage, often with red and pink margins; there are also purple leaved forms.

The massive leaves can grow to 2m (7ft) in favoured conditions, and they sprout in a fan shape from the base. A mature clump can reach 2.5m (8ft) across with six years.

The flower spikes are extraordinary, towering over the foliage by many feet, opening up into angular, red-brown parrot bill-like flowers. The flowers still manage to look attractive even when they have faded to a deep brown, almost black.

The straight species has stiff, upright leaves of dark green. The variegated form, *Phormium tenax* 'Variegatum', is marginally less hardy. It grows to 2m (6ft) tall, with striped green and cream leaves. The best form with purple leaves is *P. tenax* Pupureum Group, which grows to 1.5m (5ft). 'Nanum Purpureum' is dwarf, at 90cm (3ft) high.

There are many other named forms, many with brightly coloured foliage, but they tend to be less hardy and will revert to leaves of a single colour.

Phormium tenax

Phormium tenax 'Variegatum'

site	Full sun or light shade; good for exposed and coastal gardens
temp	Hardy, tolerating temperatures as low as -15°C (-5°F)
general care	Plant during spring; do not set central base too low, as water can collect here. Feed annually in spring
thinning	Do not disturb. Divide plants only if they are overcrowded, or if you wish to propagate
pests & diseases	Mealy bug can sometimes infest the leaves but otherwise untroubled by pests and diseases

	SPRING	SUMMER	AUTUMN	WINTER	height (cm)	spread (cm)	flower colour	
Phormium tenax	planting	flowering			200	250		Needs lots of room
P. tenax 'Nanum Purpureum'	planting	flowering			90	120		Dwarf form with purple leaves
P. tenax Purpureum Group	planting	flowering			150	150		Rich purple leaves
P. tenax 'Variegatum'	planting	flowering			200	150		Green and cream leaves

planting   flowering

Physostegia virginiana
Obedient plant

This gently spreading perennial produces well-packed flower spikes in late summer and often into early autumn, adding colour to the garden after most of the summer-flowering plants have finished.

The reason for this plant's curious common name is that the flowers are on hinged stalks, allowing them to be moved into a certain position, where they will remain, almost as if the plant is a bendy toy!

The blooms are typical of the plant family Lamiaceae (lavender, salvia and so on), coming on short flower spikes, with the many individual blooms being hooded.

The leaves have toothed edges. They are mid-green in the straight species and with a cream margin in the form *Physostegia virginiana* var. *speciosa* 'Variegata'. The

site	Grows best in bog gardens positioned in full sun or light shade
temp	Very hardy, tolerating temperatures as low as -20°C (-4°F)
general care	Plant during spring; lightly mulch plants in spring, using a light leaf mould or well-rotted garden compost
thinning	Lift and divide plants during spring, every three or four years
pests & diseases	Relatively trouble free. Pests and diseases do not usually cause any problems

Physostegia virginiana

latest variety to flower is the sugar pink *P. virginiana* 'Vivid'.

Spike-forming plants are very helpful in breaking up any tendency to uniformity in the bog garden. These, with their long flowering habit, fill such a need. Physostegia is easy to grow and is quite distinctive. They are, however, subjects that thrive in a good, loamy soil – not an inhospitable waterlogged clay.

Mulch physostegias in spring and autumn and give a balanced general fertilizer in spring. Cut down dead flowerheads once flowering has finished, and remove top growth in late autumn. Propagate by division, in spring.

P

Bog Plants

	SPRING	SUMMER	AUTUMN	WINTER	height (cm)	spread (cm)	flower colour	
Physostegia virginiana	🌱🌱🌱		●●		90	60		Likes a good, loamy soil
P. virginiana 'Alba'	🌱🌱🌱		●●		90	60		Bright white for the bog garden
P. virginiana 'Grandiflora'	🌱🌱🌱		●●		90	60		Larger flowers than the straight species
P. v. var. *speciosa* 'Bouquet Rose'	🌱🌱🌱		●●		90	60		Very old variety
P. v. var. *speciosa* 'Variegata'	🌱🌱🌱		●●		90	60		Cream variegated leaves
P. virginiana 'Summer Snow'	🌱🌱🌱		●●		90	60		Very old variety
P. virginiana 'Vivid'	🌱🌱🌱		●●		50	30		The latest to flower

  planting ● flowering

127

Primula

The primula genus ranks as one of the largest, most variable and widely appreciated of all plant genera. There are forms for growing in containers, on rockeries, in flower beds, in woodland dells and, of course, at the sides of a pond.

Bog Plants

P

Primulas are all much the same in their growing requirements, which is convenient on the one hand, but also means that if your garden does not conform to these requirements, it is unlikely that you will be able to succeed with any of them. In essence, primulas prefer sunny or lightly shaded places, and a fairly rich, organic, slightly acid soil.

Some primulas are temperamental, or elusive, but the following small selection is sure to provide colour and interest in the bog garden.

Primula japonica is possibly the best-known of the candelabra primulas, which bear their flowers in rounded clusters, or whorls, at intervals along the main central stem. It has lush leaves and several tiers of red, pink or white flowers opening at stages throughout early and mid-summer. Four of the best varieties are: 'Alba' (white), 'Apple Blossom' (pink), 'Miller's Crimson' (deep pink) and 'Postford White' (white).

Another striking candelabra is *Primula aurantiaca*, with orange or orange-red blooms that appear in late spring and early summer, which is slightly earlier than

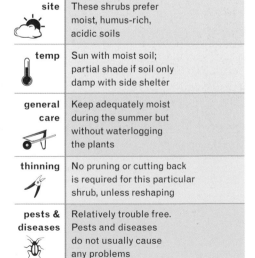

Primula beesiana

similar kinds. The flower stems reach 30cm (12in) in height.

Other candelabras include *Primula beesiana*, with rich, rosy-purple flowers; *P.* x *bulleesiana*, featuring a wide range of colours from yellow, orange and pink through to red and purple, and *P. pulverulenta*, which is pale pink or mauve.

The 'Drumstick' primula, *P. denticulata*, is extremely popular, with its neat, globular pink-purple heads 8cm (3in) across. There are many garden forms, the flower colours of which are generally given away by their varietal names: 'Glenroy Crimson'; 'Inshriach Carmine'; 'Prichard's Ruby'; 'Robinson's Red'; and 'Snowball'.

There is little that can beat a patch of *P. florindae* – the Himalayan cowslip. This plant resembles a very tall, shaggy cowslip – in the case of mature plants growing around 80cm (32in) in height – with slightly powdery, sulphur-yellow flowerheads in early summer. A smaller version of the Himalayan cowslip

Primula vialii

site	These shrubs prefer moist, humus-rich, acidic soils	
temp	Sun with moist soil; partial shade if soil only damp with side shelter	
general care	Keep adequately moist during the summer but without waterlogging the plants	
thinning	No pruning or cutting back is required for this particular shrub, unless reshaping	
pests & diseases	Relatively trouble free. Pests and diseases do not usually cause any problems	

Primula denticulata

Finally there is the lovely *P. rosea*, which does not have a common name. It is one of the earliest, and one of the tiniest of bog garden primulas. Vivid rosy pink flowers smother the ground-hugging foliage during early spring. The leaves are often bronze-tinged when young.

Primula x bulleesiana

is *P. sikkimensis*, which has its origins in the Chinese marshlands. It has bright yellow flowers in mid-spring.

One of the most stunning of all primula species is *P. vialii* – the orchid primula. It is distinct from the others in that it has startling spikes of bright red buds, and in the early part of the summer the lowest buds open to mauve or lilac blooms. The top buds are the last to open, giving the whole flowerhead an impressive dual red/lilac combination.

	SPRING			SUMMER			AUTUMN		WINTER		height (cm)	spread (cm)	flower colour	
Primula aurantiaca	🌱	🌱	🌱	✿	✿						30	30	■	Small, rosette-forming primula
P. beesiana	🌱	🌱	🌱	✿	✿						60	30	■	Sometimes difficult to find
P. x bulleesiana	🌱	🌱	🌱	✿	✿						60	30	▦	Hybrid plants in many colours
P. denticulata	🌱	🌱	🌱	✿	✿						30	30	■	One of the earliest flowering bog garden primulas
P. florindae	🌱	🌱	🌱		✿						90	45	■	Resembles large cowslips
P. japonica	🌱	🌱	🌱	✿	✿						60	30	□	Cabbage-like leaves
P. japonica 'Alba'	🌱	🌱	🌱	✿	✿						45-60	30	□	Dainty plant
P. japonica 'Apple Blossom'	🌱	🌱	🌱	✿	✿						60	30	■	Looks good next to the crimson forms
P. japonica 'Miller's Crimson'	🌱	🌱	🌱	✿	✿						60	30	■	More vigorous than straight species
P. japonica 'Postford White'	🌱	🌱	🌱	✿	✿						60	45	□	More vigorous than 'Alba'
P. pulverulenta	🌱	🌱	🌱	✿	✿						90	60	□	One of the tallest, 'hot' coloured primulas
P. rosea	🌱	🌱	🌱								15	15	□	Hugs the ground
P. sikkimensis	🌱	🌱	🌱	✿	✿	✿					75	60	□	Funnel-shaped flowers
P. vialii	🌱	🌱	🌱	✿	✿						50	30	■	Resembles a wild orchid

🌱 planting   ✿ flowering

Pulmonaria
Lungwort

A familiar and attractive hardy cottage garden perennial, Pulmonaria is often seen struggling to survive in dry borders. It is, however, much happier in moist conditions where the speckled leaves set off the pretty bright blue spring flowers.

Pulmonarias are good value, as they are often the earliest of bog garden plants to flower and later their leaves provide interesting ground cover. Needing part or full shade, they are useful for underplanting shrubs or trees in a moisture-retentive soil.

The leaves are large, rough and often prominently speckled with white, cream or silver hues. Some people have an allergic reaction to the leaves, but this is not generally a serious fault of the plant.

The main reason for growing pulmonarias is for the trumpet-shaped flowers, which fade from bright blue to red, and are held on loose heads on slightly arching stems. They appear from early to late spring.

Pulmonaria angustifolia subsp. *azurea* has intense, mid-blue flowers and the leaves are unspotted. The cultivar 'Mawson's Blue' is very similar, but with flowers of a darker blue; 'Mournful Purple' has purple flowers with silver markings on the leaves.

P. longifolia has slim, long leaves with strong silvery markings and the flowers are bright blue. Meanwhile, *P. officinalis* has silver spotted leaves and pink flowers.

Mulch plants in the autumn, as these plants do appreciate a rich, organic soil. Remove the flowerheads once the blooms start to fade or allow the blooms to set seed. Divide and replant every three or four years.

Pulmonaria angustifolia

Pulmonaria longifolia 'Bertram Anderson'

site	Grows best in bog gardens situated in light to full shade
temp	Very hardy, tolerating temperatures as low as -20°C (-4°F)
general care	Plant during the autumn, roughly 15–23cm (6–9in) apart; likes plenty of humus in the soil
thinning	Lift and divide plants during spring, every three or four years
pests & diseases	Relatively trouble free. Pests and diseases do not usually cause any problems

	SPRING	SUMMER	AUTUMN	WINTER	height (cm)	spread (cm)	flower colour	
Pulmonaria angustifolia	● ● ●		✿ ✿		30	45		Rough leaves
P. angustifolia subsp. *azurea*	● ● ●		✿ ✿		30	45		Hairy, unspotted leaves
P. longifolia 'Bertram Anderson'	● ● ●		✿ ✿		30	45		Long, slim leaves
P. 'Mawson's Blue'	● ● ●		✿ ✿		30	45		Modern hybrid
P. 'Mournful Purple'	● ● ●		✿ ✿		45	45		Modern hybrid
P. officinalis	● ● ●		✿ ✿		30	45		Silver spotted leaves

✿ planting   ● flowering

Rheum

Ornamental rhubarb

This is one of the most dramatic bog garden plants. Unlike Gunnera, which many people have likened to an ornamental rhubarb plant, Rheum really is one. Although Gunnera is much bigger, Rheum is just as impressive. The leaves, when combined with its elongated flowerheads, make it an exotic addition to the bog garden.

During late spring and early summer small, red or purple flowers appear in large plumes on rigid purplish stalks. Mature plants can grow up to 1.8m (6ft), and if you include the height of the flowerhead, 3m (10ft). Leaves are deeply lobed and rich green or purple (with a reddish tinge to the undersides). Each leaf can be 90cm (3ft) across when mature.

Rheum palmatum 'Atrosanguineum' has red spring leaves, and red flowers in summer; *R. palmatum* var. *tanguticum* has leaves that are deep green tinted purple underneath, larger and more jagged than most, and cover a 2.5m (8ft) spread.

The cultivar 'Ace of Hearts' (sometimes seen as 'Ace of Spades') is a miniature version with pink flowers and leaves that are rich red beneath.

Plant rheums in full sun or part-shade, but make sure the soil is moist and rich. Feed

Rheum palmatum

site	Grows best in bog gardens situated in full sun or light shade
temp	Hardy, tolerating temperatures as low as -15°C (5°F)
general care	Plant during spring; lightly mulch plants in spring, using a light leaf mould or well-rotted garden compost
thinning	Lift and divide plants during spring, every four or five years
pests & diseases	Relatively trouble free. Pests and diseases do not usually cause any problems

with a general fertilizer in spring. Cut down all faded flowerheads in late autumn, and cover the dormant crowns with straw or horticultural fleece. Do not let them sit in clay or waterlogged soil, as they are prone to rotting in such conditions. To propagate, divide crowns in spring; plants will need dividing every four or five years.

	SPRING	SUMMER	AUTUMN	WINTER	height (cm)	spread (cm)	flower colour	
Rheum 'Ace of Hearts'					90	750		One for the smaller bog garden
R. palmatum					300	200		Very tall when in flower
R. palmatum 'Atrosanguineum'					200	250		Blood red leaves when they first emerge
R. palmatum var. *tanguticum*					250	180		Leaves are large and jagged

 planting   flowering

Rodgersia

A noble waterside plant, this is a non-invasive clump-former from China that will grow in sun if the soil is very moist, but does tend to suffer from wind and sun scorch, so is best in part shade. It is one of those plants that look perfect next to a woodland stream or large pond, but incongruous when grown anywhere else in the garden.

The large, shining, rich green leaves of *R. aesculifolia* are evenly suffused reddish bronze, and have an intricate network of veins. They look as though they should be growing high up a horse chestnut tree (the Latin name for which is Aesculus, hence the species name), but this plant is a border perennial. Lovers of bold, dramatic, architectural plants will adore it.

In mid-summer, plumes of tiny blossoms are held well above the foliage. This plant is a classic example of the leaves being so much more important than the flowers!

All rodgersias have flowers in the pink to white colour range, but due to accidental hybridization over the years this genus contains many rather compromised species.

Rodgersia pinnata 'Superba' has deeply divided leaves and white flowers; *R. podophylla* has palm-shaped leaves and cream flowers, and *R. sambucifolia* has leaves like an elder, and white flowers.

Rodgersias need a moist soil if they are to do well. Mulch in the spring and autumn and fertilize in the spring. Leave the flowerheads in place once they are finished as the reddish seedheads come along much later in the season. Do not disturb the plants once they are established.

Rodgersia aesculifolia

Rodgersia pinnata 'Superba'

site	Grows best in bog gardens situated in sun or light shade	
temp	Hardy, tolerating temperatures as low as -15°C (5°F)	
general care	Plant during spring; lightly mulch plants in spring, using a leaf mould or well-rotted garden compost	
thinning	Lift and divide plants during spring, only when they have outgrown their space	
pests & diseases	Relatively trouble free. Pests and diseases do not usually cause any problems	

	SPRING	SUMMER	AUTUMN	WINTER	height (cm)	spread (cm)	flower colour	
Rodgersia aesculifolia	planting	flowering			120	90		Leaves resemble horse chestnut
R. pinnata	planting	flowering			90	90		Leaves arranged in pairs
R. pinnata 'Superba'	planting	flowering			90	90		Deeply divided leaves
R. podophylla	planting	flowering			90	90		Leaves rich bronze in spring
R. sambucifolia	planting	flowering			90	90		Known as the 'elder-leaved rodgersia'

 planting · flowering

Trollius
Globe flower

As long as you have a patch of soil that retains its moisture well, you can grow these eye-catching plants with ease. You will probably find three or four standard varieties in your local garden centre, but search a little harder and you will discover over 40 named forms that will provide masses of colour from mid-spring to mid-summer.

Globe flowers are incredibly hardy, and non-invasive. They are best grown in bold drifts, which is the way that they grow in the wild.

At first glance you could be forgiven for confusing trollius with the marsh marigold (*Caltha palustris*), as both are spring-flowering golden-flowered bog garden buttercups. The easiest way to tell them apart is by their leaves; Trollius have leaves that are divided and buttercup-like, whilst those of Caltha are glossy and rounded.

The original European globe flower (*Trollius europaeus*) has been tampered with by plant breeders over the years, and now there are many garden varieties available. This main species has as much charm as any of its hybrids, especially if you are growing it in a wild garden. The blooms are bright golden yellow and spherical (hence its common name). They are carried on wiry stems during late spring and early summer. The leaves are fern-like and deep green.

Most of the garden varieties have been grouped under the name *Trollius* x *cultorum*. 'Alabaster' is a very popular

hybrid with the palest of cream flowers, which appear in late spring and early summer. 'Commander in Chief' is a tallish form with spectacular glowing orange flowers, and the blooms of 'Pritchard's Giant' are orange-yellow, and go on for a very long time from late spring.

site	Performs best when grown in bog gardens that are situated in light shade
temp	Very hardy, tolerating temperatures as low as -20°C (-4°F)
general care	Plant at any time during autumn or spring; feed and lightly mulch plants in spring
thinning	Lift and divide plants during spring, every four or five years
pests & diseases	Mildew may affect leaves, but it will not cause long-term harm and often happens once flowering has finished

Trollius europaeus

Trollius chinensis is a species found in the Far East, and from which the latest hybrid has been raised. 'Golden Queen' is later flowering and slightly taller than most of the others. It will grow up to 90cm (36in).

An exceptional species from Japan is *T. hondoensis*, which has very large golden flowers with distinctive protruding yellow, petal-like stamens. As a bonus, it produces curious knobbly spiked seed capsules in late summer and autumn.

Trollius yunnanensis has wide, open, bright yellow-orange cup-shaped flowers.

The Himalayan *T. pumilis* is a departure from the above, in that it is a dwarf form at just 15cm (6in) in height, and the blooms are yellow-orange with luscious dark red exteriors.

Trollius chinensis 'Golden Queen'

Trollius x cultorum 'Orange Globe'

As wet ground can get very cold in winter, to establish trollius (as with most bog garden plants) it is better to plant them in spring, before the soil warms up. It is best to plant in groups, with 30cm (12in) between plants.

These plants tend not to perform well if they are exposed to high winds, or if exposed to the full strength of the sun all day long. Mulch around the plants in spring, and deadhead regularly (if practicable) to encourage a second flush of flowers later in the season. Give a dressing of a balanced general fertilizer in spring.

	SPRING	SUMMER	AUTUMN	WINTER	height (cm)	spread (cm)	flower colour	
Trollius chinensis 'Golden Queen'	🪏 🪏	● ●	🪏		90	45		One of the tallest hybrids
T. x cultorum 'Alabaster'	🪏 🪏 ● ●		🪏		60	45		Highly popular form
T. x cultorum 'Cheddar'	🪏 🪏 ● ●		🪏		60	45		Colour of the cheese
T. x cultorum 'Commander in Chief'	🪏 🪏 ● ●		🪏		75	45		One of the taller forms
T. x cultorum 'Fireglobe'	🪏 🪏 ● ●		🪏		60	45		Sometimes sold as 'Feuertroll'
T. x cultorum 'Lemon Queen'	🪏 🪏 ● ●		🪏		60	45		Fresh colour
T. x cultorum 'Orange Globe'	🪏 🪏 ● ●		🪏		60	45		Reliable, hardy form
T. x cultorum 'Orange Princess'	🪏 🪏 ● ●		🪏		60	45		One of the earliest to flower
T. x cultorum 'Prichard's Giant'	🪏 🪏 ● ●	●	🪏		60	45		Flowers over a long period
T. x cultorum 'Superbus'	🪏 🪏 ● ●		🪏		60	45		Large, goblet-shaped flowers
T. europaeus	🪏 🪏 ● ●		🪏		60	45		Good for a wild garden
T. hondoensis	🪏 🪏 ● ●		🪏		60	45		Spiked seed capsules in autumn
T. pumilis	🪏 🪏 ● ●		🪏		15	30		Dwarf form
T. yunnanensis	🪏 🪏 ● ●		🪏		60	45		Bright, wide, open flowers

🪏 planting   ● flowering

Ferns & Grasses

Ornamental grasses and hardy garden ferns are treated together in this section of the book. There are two main areas of similarity between these two groups of plants – at least for those species included here; firstly, none produce decorative flowers that take the eye away from the habit and form of the plant, and secondly, of course, all these plants require a moist soil.

Even a few years ago you would have been very fortunate to find more than two or three ornamental grasses listed in nursery catalogues, but in the last few years they have become the last word in garden fashion. There is now a bewildering array of species and varieties, from the architectural pampas grass to the clump forming smaller types, such as Festuca. Most members of the grass family require moist but free-draining soil.

As for ferns, every garden should have one or two of them. Few types of plant have quite such prehistoric qualities as the fern, or are as sturdy, durable and hardy. More often than not they grow in damp places although, it has to be said, a dank atmosphere is as important to them as a wet soil.

Ferns can be planted in between or in front of other plants. Try to avoid planting in positions where they will be exposed to the sun during the hottest hours of the day. Also, unless a very short fern is being grown, excessively windy situations should be avoided, to prevent wind damage to the fronds.

Ferns do not 'flower' and produce 'seeds' in the conventional sense. They reproduce by means of spores, the colonies of which are often seen as small brownish pustules on the undersides of the fronds. They make up for their lack of colour by boasting a wide variety of frond shapes and sizes, most in varying shades of green.

Carex

Carex elata 'Aurea', originally discovered growing wild in the English countryside around Norfolk by the famous gardener and plantsman E. A. Bowles (1865–1954), is one of the few sedges that is short enough, and sufficiently non-invasive, to grow in an average-sized bog garden. It does not mind having its roots in the water, either. It may be found under its incorrect name of Carex stricta 'Bowles' Golden'.

The brownish flowers of *Carex elata* 'Aurea' – separate male and female inflorescences – appear during mid-spring. Unfortunately, they are quite uninspiring. However, on the other hand, the evergreen leaves are the main reason for growing the plant. By the end of spring, after flowering, the plant throws up long, arching leaves of the strongest yellow colour of all grass-like plants, whether grown in dry soil or a bog garden. A very narrow green margin to each

site	Grows best in bog gardens situated in full sun or light shade
temp	Very hardy, tolerating temperatures as low as -20°C (-4°F)
general care	Plant during autumn or early spring; mulch plants using a leaf mould or well-rotted garden compost
thinning	Keep the clump healthy by dividing it every five or six years
pests & diseases	Relatively trouble free. Pests and diseases do not usually cause any problems

Carex elata 'Aurea'

blade makes the plant quite spectacular. The colour deepens until late summer, when it fades gradually to green.

Related plants worth considering include *Carex riparia* 'Variegata'. It is of a similar size to *C. elata* 'Aurea', and has green and white striped leaves. *C. oshimensis* 'Evergold' has broader, flattened leaves with creamy yellow variegation.

Plant this grass in full sun or light shade, setting out plants 30cm (12in) apart. Mulch in autumn and spring and give a balanced general fertilizer in spring. Leave the top growth over winter, and cut it down in early spring. Keep the clumps healthy by dividing them every five or six years; this is also the best way to propagate the plant, and this exercise should be undertaken during autumn or spring.

	SPRING	SUMMER	AUTUMN	WINTER	height (cm)	spread (cm)	flower colour	
Carex elata 'Aurea'	🌱🌸🌸		🌱		50	45		Can grow with roots in water
C. oshimensis 'Evergold'	🌱🌸🌸		🌱		50	45		Broader leaves
C. riparia 'Variegata'	🌱🌸🌸		🌱		45	45		Green/white striped leaves

 planting   🌸 flowering

Festuca glauca
Little fescue

Most people who have grown ornamental grasses would not think of the fescue family as being suitable for a bog garden. Indeed, many learned books list these plants as being more suited to dry border conditions. However, in a sunny place, on a moist soil that is not permanently waterlogged, these little grasses will do very well.

The Festuca genus contains some fifty or so species and cultivars, and whereas most come in shades of green, there are some excellent blue and golden leaved forms. The most popular of the little blue fescues is *Festuca glauca* 'Elijah Blue'. This makes evergreen rounded cushions some 30cm (12in) tall, with soft needle-like leaves that are an intense silvery-blue in summer, and greener in winter. In late spring and early summer it produces slender panicles, the stems and flowers being exactly the same colour as the leaves, though both become biscuit brown as the flowers turn to seeds.

Festuca glauca minima is notable for growing only to around 10cm (4in) in height, and it has attractive, wiry little leaves of a very pale blue. Meanwhile the cultivar 'Azurit' is taller and less silvery.

Festuca glauca 'Golden Toupee' forms tight cushions some 23cm (9in) across, of soft, needle-like leaves that are almost iridescent yellow in spring, later fading to a yellowish green. As with the blue form, the flowers are the same colour as the leaves, but turning beige or brown as they fade.

All forms of *F. glauca* are useful for edging or as foreground groups, either massed or spaced as small specimens. Best foliage colour is maintained by dividing the clumps every two or three years.

site	Grows best in moist soils – but not waterlogged – in full sun
temp	Very hardy, tolerating temperatures as low as -20°C (-4°F)
general care	Plant during spring at the front of a border; in spring lightly mulch and apply a general fertilizer
thinning	Lift and divide plants during spring, every two or three years
pests & diseases	Relatively trouble free. Pests and diseases do not usually cause any problems

Festuca glauca 'Elijah Blue'

Festuca glauca 'Golden Toupee'

	SPRING	SUMMER	AUTUMN	WINTER	height (cm)	spread (cm)	flower colour	
Festuca glauca	🌱🌱🌱✿	✿			30	30		Densely tufted, bluey-green
F. glauca 'Azurit'	🌱🌱🌱✿	✿			35	45		Taller than most
F. glauca 'Elijah Blue'	🌱🌱🌱✿	✿			30	60		Bluest of all fescues
F. glauca 'Golden Toupee'	🌱🌱🌱✿	✿			30	60		Leaves turn to yellow-green
F. glauca minima	🌱🌱🌱✿	✿			10	15		Smallest blue fescue

 planting   flowering

Glyceria maxima var. variegata

Striped manna grass *or* Variegated sweet grass

This is the perfect waterside grass if you have lots of room in your garden. Its natural home is at the sides of streams and rivers throughout Europe and Asia, where its aggressive nature means that it can grow unbounded. If your garden is medium sized or smaller, you should not attempt to grow it unless you are prepared to restrain it regularly by lifting and dividing.

Despite its somewhat rampant nature, this is, however, one of the most beautifully variegated of all grasses, both when viewed from close up and from a distance. The soft, blunt-tipped leaves, which can be as much as 60cm (2ft) long and some 5cm (2in) across, are cream, narrowly green-striped and tinged with a pink flush in spring. In autumn, just before the leaves fade away, they take on purple tints. Vivid, mid-year colouring can be so dramatic that Glyceria needs handling with care, or it will dominate all surrounding plants.

The flowers, which are borne from mid-summer until early autumn, are open, heavily branched and creamy-white.

The clump grows to 60cm (2ft) in height, but when the flowers are in season, the stalks that bear them can rise to a height of 90cm (3ft). Glyceria associates well with such bog garden plants as astilbes, candelabra primulas and waterside ferns. The cream of the leaves goes exceptionally well with bluish-leaved plants, so grow it with *Festuca glauca* 'Elijah Blue' or, for an attractive contrast in leaf shape as well as colour, *Hosta* 'Bressingham Blue'.

A 'yellow' bog garden can be a very dramatic feature. Such an area could contain Glyceria, along with *Carex elata* 'Aurea' and even *Iris pseudacorus*, for its vivid golden flowers. Propagate the species by seed or division; the cultivar only by division.

Glyceria maxima var. variegata

site	Grows best in water gardens situated in full sun or light shade
temp	Very hardy, tolerating temperatures as low as -20°C (-4°F)
general care	Plant during spring; apply a mulch for the plants in autumn and spring, until they are established
thinning	Lift and divide overgrown plants at any time, as they can spread indefinitely
pests & diseases	Relatively trouble free. Pests and diseases do not usually cause any problems

Hakonechloa

This is a soft-leaved and frequently variegated herbaceous grass, originally from the area around Hakone in Honshu, Japan. It is the perfect plant for the smaller garden, as it is slow-growing, compact and non-invasive which are among the reasons why this plant is so popular.

Hakonechloa can be a most striking plant when the sun shines on its brightly coloured leaves. Its size and grace make it attractively informal, yet its arching leaves and hemispherical shape conspire to give it almost perfect symmetry, making it ideal for the formal garden as well.

The flowers come as open panicles of reddish-brown spikes – fairly insignificant – in early autumn, and they last well into winter.

The leaves are yellow and white on a pale green base; they gradually turn to a reddish-brown as they age. The leaf stems are purplish. This grass, which may be found in some nurseries under its old name of *Hakonechloa macra* 'Variegata', looks particularly good when planted next to a large-leaved and

site	Performs best when grown in bog gardens situated in light shade
temp	With shelter from cold, drying winds, will tolerate as low as -20°C (-4°F)
general care	Plant during spring; lightly mulch in spring and autumn, and apply a general fertilizer in spring
thinning	Lift and divide plants during spring, every three or four years
pests & diseases	Relatively trouble free. Pests and diseases do not usually cause any problems

contrasting-coloured plant, such as the blue-leaved *Hosta* 'Hadspen Blue'.

Another superbly variegated form is *H. macra* 'Aureola', with striking golden yellow stripes on a bright green base. A reddish flush usually suffuses the leaves as autumn arrives.

The common species *H. macra* is in itself not unattractive, with its simple and graceful mid-green leaves.

These grasses are tolerant of light shade – in fact, this will enhance their colouring. Plant directly into the soil in the bog garden, during spring. If planting more than one of these grasses, do not place them closer together than 25cm (10in). Mulch around the plants in autumn and spring, and give a dressing of a balanced general fertilizer in spring.

Divide congested plants every three or four years. This should be carried out in spring or autumn.

Hakonechloa macra 'Aureola'

	SPRING	SUMMER	AUTUMN	WINTER	height (cm)	spread (cm)	flower colour	
Hakonechloa macra	planting		flowering		40	60		Straight green leaves
H. macra 'Alboaurea'	planting		flowering		40	60		Yellow and white leaves
H. macra 'Aureola'	planting		flowering		20	30		Bright yellow leaves with green stripes

 planting   *flowering*

Matteuccia

Matteuccia has a reputation for being a bit of a thug in the garden, as it will spread almost indefinitely if it is happy with its soil and surrounding environment. You will need space to appreciate its shape and form, and to accommodate its eagerness to put out runners and establish new plants.

site	These ferns grow best around water gardens that are situated in light shade	
temp	Very hardy, tolerating temperatures as low as -20°C (-4°F)	
general care	Plant during spring; cut away dead foliage in the autumn; mulch around roots each spring	
thinning	Lift unwanted plants at any time, as these ferns can spread indefinitely	
pests & diseases	Relatively trouble free. Pests and diseases do not usually cause any problems	

Matteuccia struthiopteris

Matteuccia struthiopteris is a deciduous fern, dying back completely in late autumn. In spring you cannot fail to be impressed by the masses of new, infertile leaves that are produced, unfurling from a basal rosette around central, dark brown permanent fertile fronds. They are the freshest of lime green hues and look good spotlighted by shafts of early morning sunshine.

The closely related *Matteuccia orientalis* produces lance-shaped fronds, initially green but soon turning brown. The spreading nature of this fern's foliage makes it a very distinctive garden plant. It is a pretty fern and deserves to be grown more widely.

Provided the soil is moist, shuttlecock ferns will be perfectly happy. They can cope with most soil types but will benefit from plenty of organic matter around their roots. For lush, vigorous growth, apply a spring dressing of a balanced fertilizer.

Remove the old, dead fronds in spring so that they do not interfere with the current season's new growth. Mulch the area around the roots with well-rotted compost each spring, to build up a moist, nutrient-rich soil.

Propagation is not usually an issue with Matteuccia, as it has a natural willingness to spread. Plants put out runners or rhizomes that travel just beneath the soil surface. These do not produce occasional fronds along their length, unlike many ferns. Instead, they produce complete baby plants. If carefully lifted with a spade and fork, each one of these can be moved to a more suitable position – or left where it is to help produce a mature swathe of foliage all around the parent plant.

	SPRING	SUMMER	AUTUMN	WINTER	height (cm)	spread (cm)	flower colour
Matteuccia orientalis					90	100+	Foliage soon turns brown
M. struthiopteris					150	100+	Likes a humus-rich soil

🌱 *planting*

Milium effusum

Golden wood millet *or* Bowles' golden grass

The most golden form of this plant, 'Aureum', is an excellent lightener of semi-shaded places in the garden, and is a real gem of spring and early summer. It is a loosely growing tufted perennial with soft, limp leaves growing to an overall height of some 30cm (12in).

Every above-ground part of the plant is bright yellow: the broad, soft, somewhat floppy leaves, the flowering stems, and the open panicles of tiny spikelets on hair-fine branches in early summer. It has a slightly greener appearance as the season progresses, or if it is grown in too much shade.

The normal species is a European woodland grass of no real garden merit, and for this reason it may be hard to find. The golden form of this plant is immeasurably more attractive.

Although this can be a short-lived plant, fading after three or four years, when it is well suited to its conditions it will self-seed happily. It looks particularly good between green or yellow variegated shrubs.

Do not confuse this, Bowles' golden grass, with *Carex elata* 'Aurea' (Bowles' golden sedge).

Milium effusum 'Aureum'

site	Grows best around a water garden situated in light shade
temp	Very hardy, tolerating temperatures as low as -20°C (-4°F)
general care	Plant during spring; lightly mulch plants in autumn and spring, and apply a general fertilizer in spring
thinning	Lift and divide overgrown plants when necessary
pests & diseases	Relatively trouble free. Pests and diseases do not usually cause any problems

Enrich the soil around these plants by mulching in both spring and autumn, and feed in spring with a balanced, general fertilizer. Allow the leaves to die down naturally after flowering.

Unless you want to propagate them by division, it is best to leave established plants alone as they usually resent disturbance and do not respond well to being moved around the garden.

	SPRING	SUMMER	AUTUMN	WINTER	height (cm)	spread (cm)	flower colour	
Milium effusum	🌱🌱🌱	☀☀	🌱🌱		30	50	☐	Stunning green leaf standing out from the rest
M. effusum 'Aureum'	🌱🌱🌱	☀☀	🌱🌱		30	50	▨	Fairly short-lived plant
M. effusum var. *esthonicum*	🌱🌱🌱	☀☀	🌱🌱		35	45	☐	Aromatic leaves when crushed

 planting ☀ flowering

Onoclea sensibilis

There is just one recognized species in the Onoclea genus, but this one plant represents one of the best and most distinctive of ferns for general cultivation, so it is well worth tracking down and cultivating in the water garden.

This is a robust, deciduous, low-growing fern with crowded triangular, light blue-green fronds. The fertile fronds are quite dissimilar, with spore-bearing 'sporangia' being formed into bunches like so many beads or bunches of small grapes. It will flourish by the waterside where it will run about to form considerable colonies, the fronds often lasting quite late into the end of the year before being seen off by hard frosts. While usually it has green stems during the growing season, there is a form with reddish stems. Although the red colouring is at its strongest in spring, there is a hint of it all year. This red form does not have a registered name, and simply goes by the epithet *Onoclea sensibilis* – copper.

This plant grows from creeping underground rhizomes, which means that it spreads – very rapidly in wet ground – and therefore may become a little invasive in small gardens. However, its distinct foliage usually makes it a welcome invader.

Onoclea is called the 'sensitive fern' because it dies down with the first frost in autumn. Interestingly, late spring frosts do not appear to be so damaging.

Originally from northern Asia and North America, Onoclea will not take too kindly to a chalky or alkaline soil; acid to neutral conditions are its preferences.

Propagate by division. Alternatively, the green spores ripen in mid-winter and can be induced to shed in a heated room in around half an hour. Spores need to be sown as soon as possible after shedding.

site	Grows best in a water garden situated in light to medium shade
temp	Very hardy, tolerating temperatures as low as -20°C (-4°F)
general care	Plant during spring; mulch plants in spring, using a leaf mould or well-rotted garden compost
thinning	Peel back rhizomes near the soil surface from unwanted areas
pests & diseases	Relatively trouble free. Pests and diseases do not usually cause any problems

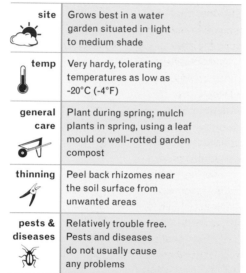

Onoclea sensibilis

Osmunda

Arguably the most impressive of all the hardy deciduous ferns, Osmunda was once common in the wild wet fens and marsh banks of Europe, but is now most often seen in gardens. It is a highly desirable plant for large bog gardens, and is very vigorous and spreading, although some of the cultivated forms are less demanding of space.

Lime green, prettily divided fronds first appear as copper-tinted crooked shoots in spring, finally turning a brilliant yellow and bronze in autumn. Smaller, stiffer spore-bearing fronds arise from the centre of the plant.

Osmunda regalis 'Purpurascens' has purple-green stems and fronds, and markedly pink-brown young shoots. 'Cristata' (the crested royal fern) is smaller, and has attractively tasselled foliage.

Osmunda claytoniana (the interrupted fern) derives its common name from the spores that are borne around the stalk in a part of the frond that is devoid of leaflets. Leaflets above and below this spore area develop quite normally, giving the entire frond the appearance of having been interrupted.

In spring, plant single, specimen plants in full sun, or light to moderate shade. The ideal soil is moist and acid, with plenty of humus. Mulch with garden compost after planting, and annually every spring, feeding with a general fertilizer at the same time.

It is advisable to leave the dead fronds in place at the end of autumn, so that they protect the emerging young fertile fronds in spring. Cut the dead foliage back in spring.

Divide congested clumps in spring, or sow ripe spores under glass in autumn or spring.

Osmunda claytoniana

Osmunda regalis

site	Grows best in areas of full sun or light to moderate shade
temp	Very hardy, tolerating temperatures as low as -20°C (-4°F)
general care	Plant during spring; lightly feed and mulch plants with garden compost after planting
thinning	Divide congested clumps; chopping off small portions may be all that is possible
pests & diseases	Relatively trouble free. Pests and diseases do not usually cause any problems

	SPRING	SUMMER	AUTUMN	WINTER	height (cm)	spread (cm)	flower colour
Osmunda claytoniana	🌱 🌱 🌱				90	90	A fascinating, easy-to-establish fern
O. regalis	🌱 🌱 🌱				200	180	Copper tinted green, turning yellow and bronze in autumn
O. regalis 'Cristata'	🌱 🌱 🌱				120	120	The tips of the fronds are flat crested
O. regalis 'Purpurascens'	🌱 🌱 🌱				210	180	Purple-green stems and fronds

 planting

Pennisetum
Fountain grass

Grasses in the Pennisetum genus generally feature bristly flowers resembling bottle brushes or hairy caterpillars. The forms covered here are clump-forming grasses with good, green foliage some 75cm (30in) tall, and perhaps as much as 90cm (3ft) across. The flowers of these plants, which look like browny pink foxtails, are borne in late summer on slender arching stems all over the clump, and it is these that create the fountain effect honoured by the common name.

When in flower, fountain grass can stand as high as 1m (39in), and often taller still in very warm climes. In cool, dull summers there may not be such a good show of flowers, which is why several cultivars were introduced to fill this need. 'Woodside' is probably the best, and shorter than the species. 'Weserbergland' has a similar smaller stature, but with greeny white flowers. 'Cassian' has notable autumn colouring, and reaches 60cm (2ft) with a slightly wider spread.

'Little Bunny' is small at 30cm (12in) when in flower, whilst 'Hameln' is slightly larger, growing to some 45cm (18in).

In most temperate parts of the world *Pennisetum orientale* (the oriental fountain grass) will start to produce flowers around mid-summer and continue until the first frosts.

All of these are plants best grown in a sunny spot, in soil that is consistently moist. Propagate by division.

Pennisetum alopecuroides

Pennisetum setaceum

site	Grows best in moist but not waterlogged soil in full sun
temp	Hardy, tolerating temperatures as low as -15°C (5°F)
general care	Plant during spring; give some protection from the worst of the winter cold
thinning	Lift and divide plants during spring, every three or four years
pests & diseases	Relatively trouble free. Pests and diseases do not usually cause any problems

	SPRING	SUMMER	AUTUMN	WINTER	height (cm)	spread (cm)	flower colour	
Pennisetum alopecuroides	🌱🌱🌱	●	●		90	75		Good, green foliage
P. alopecuroides 'Cassian'	🌱🌱🌱	●	●		60	75		Foliage turns russet in autumn
P. alopecuroides 'Hameln'	🌱🌱🌱	●	●		45	50		Free-flowering
P. alopecuroides 'Little Bunny'	🌱🌱🌱	●	●		30	45		The smallest form
P. alopecuroides 'Weserbergland'	🌱🌱🌱	●	●		75	75		Good flower colour
P. alopecuroides 'Woodside'	🌱🌱🌱	●	●		60	75		Often regarded as the best
P. setaceum	🌱🌱🌱	● ●	●		90	45		Purplish-pink spikelets

🌱 planting   ● flowering

Schoenoplectus lacustris
Club rush

This is one of the many aquatic rushes, widespread throughout the northern hemisphere, growing in damp soil along the edges of streams and rivers. As a garden plant it provides a mass of useful greenery, but lacks interest.

Even more attractive are the striking variegated forms, the names of which are real mouthfuls: *Schoenoplectus lacustris* subsp. *tabernaemontani* 'Albescens' (with white stems and longitudinal green stripes), and *S. lacustris* subsp. *tabernaemontani* 'Zebrinus', (green stems and horizontal pale cream stripes). The round stems and grass-like leaves of both these forms can be good talking points.

The stems are hollow and delicate, making them susceptible to damage by strong winds and mishandling; they will easily bend and then look unsightly. When this happens, a clean, surgical cut just below the bend will improve the appearance.

These variegated rushes often revert to the basic, all-green form. If this happens, remove any that are seen as soon as possible. The cream-white parts of the variegations can sometimes fade a little in high summer; if it is growing in a shady spot, this fading is less pronounced.

The insignificant green-brown flowers are produced at the tips of the stems, but actually appear to be carried at the side, about three-quarters of the way up. This is because two bracts extend upwards past the flower and appear to be a continuation of the stem.

These plants appreciate being fed with a general fertilizer in spring, and respond by producing beautifully marked, lush growth in quantity.

To propagate, divide the tough, wiry root system. This is best carried out in spring, using a sharp knife to cut straight down through the root mass. Replant the small sections straight away into permanently moist soil – or even mud.

You may still find these plants for sale under the old name of *Scirpus lacustris*.

site	Grows best in moist areas in full sun or light shade
temp	Hardy, tolerating temperatures as low as -15°C (5°F)
general care	Plant during spring. Allow stems and leaves to die down naturally before tidying dead top-growth
thinning	Lift and divide overcrowded plants at any time
pests & diseases	Relatively trouble free. Pests and diseases do not usually cause any problems

Schoenoplectus lacustris

	SPRING	SUMMER	AUTUMN	WINTER	height (cm)	spread (cm)	flower colour	
Schoenoplectus lacustris	planting	flowering			150	45		Brown seed heads
S. l. subsp. tabernaemontani 'Albescens'	planting	flowering			180	45		Longitudinal green stripes
S. l. subsp. tabernaemontani 'Zebrinus'	planting	flowering			180	45		Horizontal cream stripes

 planting   *flowering*

Planting Combinations

It is immediately obvious, to even the most casual observer let alone the serious and experienced gardener, that some plants do not sit comfortably with others. Perhaps they both have small leaves of a similar green colouring; in this case, you would find it difficult to see where one plant ends and another one begins. Similarly, if the flowers are of the same colour, or with only a very slight difference in hues, there will be a visual clash, with a mish-mash of textures and light, and the whole effect will be less than satisfactory.

So, how should we plan a planting scheme in and around the pond, which looks good from the moment we conceive it until the full realization of it in the garden?

Understanding foliage

Although the success of any planting combination is ultimately a matter of personal preference, it is generally accepted throughout the global gardening community that the best plant combinations are those in which, for example, large bold leaves (such as hostas, rodgersias or lysichitons) are sited next to finer-foliaged plants (such as astilbes, primulas or even irises). Similarly, because of the considerable difference between the shapes of the leaves, an attractive grass-like plant will sit very well next to a bold broad-leaved plant.

The colours of the leaves also plays an important role. For example, a plant with 'normal' green leaves can be enhanced by its being placed next to a plant with variegated leaves. Similarly, the variegated plant will stand out when surrounded by plants which have plain coloured leaves.

Placing blue-leaved plants, such as *Hosta* 'Hadspen Blue' or *Festuca glauca* 'Elijah Blue' next to, or in the vicinity of, yellow-leaved plants such as *Hosta* 'Gold Edger' or *Carex elata* 'Aurea' can achieve a really pleasing combination.

One plant that tends always to be better placed on its own, as a specimen plant, is *Houttuynia cordata* 'Chameleon'. It has so many colours and shades in its leaves that it does not really 'go' with any other plant. This should not, however, deter you from growing it, as it is beautiful in its own right.

Getting the timing right

One of the first points to be aware of when planning a border or a planting scheme is the periods when certain plants do certain things. It is usually the aim of the gardener to grow as wide a variety of plants as possible, and to achieve colour and effect for as much of the year as possible. This will usually manifest itself in 'pockets' of colour over a long season, rather than a carnival of colour over a month or so, with nothing going on throughout the rest of the year.

Specifically, to grow a plant that flowers in early spring is perfectly acceptable, but to place it between two other plants that flower in early spring is perhaps a waste. There will already be a degree of colour in that part of the pond or bog garden, so why not place this new subject somewhere else entirely, somewhere perhaps that is lacking colour at that time?

The flowering time of neighbouring plants is also critical if their colours are the same or similar. For example, a mid-summer flowering pink Astilbe next to a mid-summer flowering orange Hemerocallis would not be a good idea, as they both flower at the same time and the two colours clash. A mid-summer flowering pink Astilbe next to a late spring flowering orange Hemerocallis would be better, as the two plants will not be competing with each other for your attention.

Contrasts in plant colour and form are as important in the water garden as anywhere else

Use of the water and surroundings

Because we are concentrating on planting ponds, water features and bog gardens, we are not going to have the same problems of scale that are experienced in some other parts of the garden. It is not a good idea to site tall trees and large shrubs near to a pond, because they cast shade over the water, which prohibits good aquatic plant and animal development.

But at the planning stage, planting near to or in the water can have its own sets of problems. Throughout this book we have examined which plants need to have their roots in water, and which merely prefer moist soil. It is critical to have this knowledge at the planning stage. It is also important to know which plants will grow upright and which will hang over the pond edge or even drape into the water.

Waterlilies, for example, have virtually no above-water height, and so you can plant them anywhere in the pond and they will not spoil other plants. However, after a couple of years a vigorous waterlily can swamp other, less aggressive, varieties. Another point to bear in mind with waterlilies is that they do not like to be placed near fountains or waterfalls, as the constant water movement is debilitating to them.

One of the most attractive things about water is its ability to reflect. Reflection is a dimension unavailable in any other aspect of gardening, so we should exploit it. The reflection of plants growing in and around the pond can be enjoyed almost as much as the real above-water scene. A strategically placed garden ornament, bird-bath, sundial or similar structure can also be repeated in a watery reflection. But beware, so too can ugly nearby buildings or, if you are not careful, even the neighbour's washing line!

Fish, Koi & Wildlife

A pond is not complete if it does not have some fish or wildlife thriving in it and, in their own way, decorating it; these creatures add colour and animation, particularly in formal pools. Fish can also significantly reduce the number of midges and mosquitoes that frequent a garden.

The fish with the best social mastery are the koi (full name: *nishikigoi*). They feed from your hand readily and, over a period of time, develop wonderful characteristics. Although koi are descendants of the common carp, their selective breeding over the years has meant that they are much more particular about their water conditions. To keep even one single koi successfully, you should provide filtration, water movement and oxygenation, year-round care, special food and, of course, high water quality. The hobby requires investment and dedication.

Keeping large koi in planted 'ornamental' ponds can, however, present problems. This is because koi are voracious creatures that will tear plants to pieces and because large-leafed plants such as waterlilies will act as hiding places, preventing the koi from being seen.

Water volume and depth are very important to the koi as both have a significant bearing on body size and shape development. Koi can grow over 60cm (24in) in length, so even a beginner's pond should have a volume of no less than, say, 13,638 l (3000 gal). Ideally, the depth of the pond should be 1.35m (4ft 6in) or more.

Attracting and maintaining a wildlife presence, however, is cheap, easy, and provides as much enjoyment and fascination as anything else in water gardening. Flying insects such as beetles and dragonflies are some of the first inhabitants in any new pond, and amphibians like frogs and toads appear as if from nowhere. Single-celled creatures are often carried on the wind from one pond to another.

Buying Pond Fish

The urge to install fish in a new pond can be enormous. Resist it! Six weeks is not an unrealistic time to wait. During the first couple of weeks, fresh water in the pond will turn brown-green as micro-organisms multiply. A variety of plants should be put in place, including submerged oxygenators. These will help to absorb dissolved minerals, and of course provide oxygen to the water. The fish will need these plants for both protection and as a source of green food. By the sixth week the water should be clear.

Buying some fish from a garden centre, transporting them home, and then putting them in the pond – with no forethought about the environment they were in or the one to which they are about to be subjected – can result in a high mortality rate.

TIP

Before you buy pond fish you should know how many, and of what size, your pond can accommodate safely. This is a good guide: allow 155sq cm (24sq in) of water surface area per 2.5cm (1in) length of fish – excluding tails! Once the calculation has been made, reduce it by 25%, to allow for the fish to grow.

SELECTING FISH FOR YOUR POND

You take a gamble when buying fish – nobody can say with 100% conviction whether a fish is absolutely free of disease or parasites, regardless of how healthy it may look. This guide may be useful:

The swimming technique. A healthy fish should swim at a regular pace, in straight lines, and in a considered way. It should not roll about, or lose its balance, or keep floating upwards, or sinking downwards.

A lively disposition. Goldfish, orfe and koi should be constantly on the move, and even dart about when 'spooked'. If they seem lethargic, or float on the surface, or lie relatively still at the bottom, then they are best avoided.

The body. If you see blood spots, or fungal growth (resembling cottonwool), then do not buy any fish from the same tank. Damaged or missing scales are unsightly, but not necessarily a sign of ill-health.

The fins. A healthy fish should have its fins well extended. Any damaged fins will indicate that the fish has been in a scrap, and it should be avoided.

The colour. A protective layer of mucus, which tends to enhance the colour of the fish, making the body bright, vivid and clear, covers the scales of a fish. If the fish is unhealthy, its scales will often be dull or cloudy in general appearance.

The eyes. A healthy fish should have clear eyes. If they are 'milky' in appearance, it is a possible sign that the fish is injured or otherwise unhealthy.

Take your time when buying fish. It is important to select the healthiest specimens

Introducing fish to the pond

When you buy fish from a pet shop or aquatic centre, and then transport them home, they will be subjected to a considerable degree of stress. If the journey home is likely to take longer than four hours, the bag containing the fish should be opened in order for more oxygen to be made available to them. Fish are highly sensitive to changes in temperature and water quality, so avoid any shocks when transferring them to the pond. When you buy fish from a pet shop or aquatic centre they will be given to you in a plastic bag. For best results, follow this simple process:

1. Place the bag containing the fish in the pond, and leave it for 10 minutes so that the water temperature inside the bag reduces to the same as that of the pond water.
2. Introduce a little pond water into the bag. Leave it to stand for 10 minutes.
3. Add a little more water and leave for a further 10 minutes.
4. Push the bag on to its side so that the fish can swim away freely.

Hardy Pond Fish Species

The common goldfish is a fairly long-lived fish – a lifespan of 15 years is not unusual – and millions are bred annually by fish farms, which also makes them cheap to buy.

Originally from China and parts of Siberia, the goldfish is a hardy breed, able to withstand temperatures practically down to freezing. It can grow to 30cm (12in) from head to tail, if the conditions are right, and the pool large enough. Fancy varieties are generally considerably smaller. The 'normal' goldfish is short-finned, usually orange but is available in other single colour variations.

'Normal' goldfish are short-finned

These are some of the most commonly seen types of pond fish:

Shubunkins A graceful fish with large fins. The Bristol Shubunkin is single-tailed, long-finned and with mottled coloration which normally includes a little blue.

Comet A sleeker cousin of the shubunkin, with a longer tail, often pointed.

Veiltail Oval-bodied double-tailed with long, flowing fins.

Ranchu Oval-bodied, with a curved back profile minus the dorsal fin. Usually orange.

Moor Double-tailed black fish, sometimes with protruding eyes, rather more tender than the others.

Fantail and Oranda are tender and at their best in a coldwater aquarium. However, they make good pond inhabitants for the warmer months.

Golden orfe Perfect for larger ponds, the wild orfe is silver, but the golden form has been bred for use in garden ponds, along with blue and marbled variants. These fish are fast movers, and seem to enjoy the splashes from fountains.

Golden orfe are good for big ponds

Golden tench This fish can grow to 71cm (28in), although 30–41cm (12–16in) is more usual for a healthy adult in a large domestic pond. Tench are excellent scavengers and feed off the muddy bottoms of the pond.

Golden rudd Silver, with a golden hue, their scales are large and rough-looking, and make identification fairly easy. In a pond the rudd can grow to 41cm (16in), feeding on worms, insects and aquatic vegetation.

Grass carp Most kept in ornamental pools are albinos, which are attractive against dark sided ponds. They can get large – over 1m (3ft) in length – so a large pond is required.

Feeding

Fish are generally omnivorous, naturally eating both plant and animal material, some types scouring the bottom of the pond for worms, shrimps, algae and even decaying matter.

Do not give your fish artificial feed (flakes or pellets) if the temperature drops below 7°C (45°F). It is harmful to feed fish when it is so cold as their metabolic processes, including digestion, slow right down, increasing the danger of food rotting inside the gut. When the water temperature stabilizes above 15°C (59°F), high protein, growth-inducing feed can be used.

Your fish will live longer when fed specialist food

Keeping Koi

Great pleasure is gained from seeing koi swimming in clear, clean water, watching them grow and their patterns change as they develop. Newcomers to koi keeping should spend time with fellow hobbyists or dealers: this is the best way to learn about the types of fish, the care they need, and the types of products needed to keep them healthy. Here we offer only a basic introduction to the hobby.

These fish are expensive to buy, particularly if they are brought home to inadequate facilities, and die as a result. The correct facilities, including an adequate filter, must be in place before buying commences.

Identifying koi

Because Japan is the home of the koi, and this is where much of the breeding has taken place, koi are regularly referred to globally by their Japanese classes and variety names. The following is a simplified list of the various classes of metallic and non-metallic koi; the distinction between one class and another can be blurred, and even experts are regularly baffled:

METALLIC

Hikarimono Single-coloured metallic koi often in gold, silver, yellow, orange, grey and platinum variations.
Hikarimoyomono Metallic orange or yellow on white.
Hikariutsurimono Metallic forms of Utsuri and Showa.
Sanshoko koi (see below).

NON-METALLIC

Kohaku Red markings on a white base.
Tancho Sanke Red and black markings on a white base.

A non-metallic Kohaku koi

Showa Sanshoko Red and white markings on a black base.
Bekko Black markings on a red, yellow or white base colour.
Utsurimono Red, yellow or white markings on a black base colour.
Asagi and Shusui Body blue or dark blue, with red/orange belly.
Koromo Red markings overlaid with darker pattering, on a white base colour.

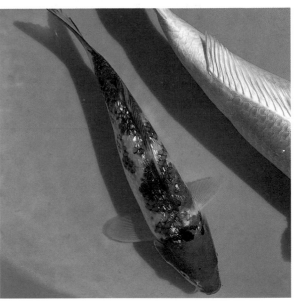

Tancho Single red spot on the top of the head.
Kawarimono All other forms of non-metallic koi, including single colours.
Kinginrin Fish having shiny scales of any body type.

Requirements for avoiding koi 'stress'

Koi must live in a stress-free environment. There are many factors involved in fish stressing, such as:
Pollutants The water should be chemically clean – do this by installing a biological filter of adequate size for the volume of fish population in the pond. It is essential to use a water testing kit to ensure that the effect of fish respiration and waste have not made the water toxic because of increased ammonia or nitrite levels.
Oxygen The circulation of water via some form of water course to help aerate the water will normally provide sufficient oxygen for your koi, but most koi keepers incorporate a venturi, or an air pump, into their system.
Vitamins and minerals These must be supplemented by feeding good quality food, formulated for koi.
Heavy metals There should be low, or preferably zero, levels of the heavy metals such as lead, copper and zinc; these can restrict growth, prevent reproduction and cause death if allowed to accumulate in the body. Your mains water supplier will be able to give you information on heavy metal levels in the supply.
Temperature Variable levels can seriously affect the koi; keepers often add some form of heating to their pond system to achieve stability of temperature.

Encouraging Wildlife

In a balanced garden there should be a stable food chain of prey and predator. For example, destroying all of the greenfly in a garden will deprive ladybirds and blue tits of food. And a garden without any slugs at all is unlikely to have any frogs or toads (even if there is a pond). Low populations of most pests should be tolerated, and will help to encourage wildlife.

Amphibious wildlife

Frogs These are possibly our most welcome visitors, roaming the garden devouring slugs and other garden pests as they go. Sometimes heavy frog populations can 'bully' residential fish, but this does not usually become a serious problem. Adults spend most of the summer living in moist, shaded vegetation, but never far from the water.

From late winter, frogs begin their spawning rituals. Soon glutinous clumps of spawn are seen, and within weeks these turn into thousands of tadpoles. These feed on pond algae initially, but then as they age they turn carnivore and eat small pond-dwelling invertebrates, including each other!

Toads Mainly nocturnal feeders, common and natterjack toads are usually larger, wartier, rarer and more rounded in shape than frogs. They can hibernate up to a mile away from the spawning pond, under piles of leaves and in holes in the soil. These will eat slugs, caterpillars, beetles, woodlice and even ants. Mid- to late spring is when you will see see strings of eggs, wound around the submerged pondweed.

Newts Smooth, crested and palmate newts are shy, secretive creatures, but they are just as beneficial as frogs and toads in terms of eating garden pests. It is not easy to identify between the species, as there are times of year when one species can closely resemble another.

Newts emerge from hibernation – generally from under pondside vegetation or large, flat stones – around mid-spring. Eggs are laid individually, usually in submerged foliage.

Leeches The most unpopular of all pond inhabitants, they suck the bodily fluids out of their prey. They are also fairly unpleasant looking, with black, wriggling bodies. To avoid getting leeches in your pond, check any plants or fish you introduce – wherever they come from. Most species feed on water snails and fish.

Frogs are a boon in the water garden – definitely the gardener's friend

Insects

Damselflies and dragonflies The larvae of these beautiful creatures live under the water (for as long as five years in the case of some dragonflies), feeding on small creatures passing by. They gradually climb out of the pond to emerge as adults. Damselflies are slightly daintier versions of the dragonfly, and it is possible to find red and blue versions of both. Both insects are found naturally wherever there is a large body of water.

Pond skaters You cannot fail to recognize these endearing insects. They 'walk' on the surface of the water, spreading their weight over as large an area as possible. They feed on dead and dying insects, and effectively 'clean-up' the surface of the water for us, albeit on a minuscule scale.

There are 10 species; some with wings will quickly fly in and inhabit a new pond, whilst others must be carried to their new home on plants.

Water boatman This familiar bug – actually a type of fly – swims just beneath the surface of the water, using its legs and body like a boat being powered by oars. There are two main types: the lesser water boatman, which sieves organic matter from the water via hairs on its legs (it also uses its legs to rub together at mating time, rather like the grasshopper); and the greater water boatman, which is a predator, and can even bite!

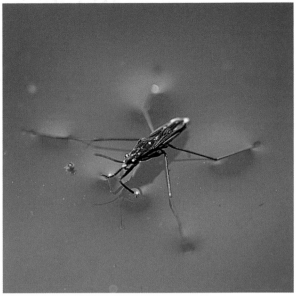

Pond skaters serve a useful purpose in cleansing the water surface

Mosquitoes These pests prefer still waters to ponds with waterfalls and fountains; they lay eggs anywhere that is still, even in long-standing puddles and waterbutts. Fortunately the eggs and larvae are considered delicious by fish; you will therefore often find greater populations of mosquitoes wherever there is an absence of fish.

Mammals, birds and others

A host of mammals will come to your pond to partake of its delights. Many of these creatures will arrive at night, so you will not always see them. Their presence, however, forms part of the rich diversity that makes keeping a wildlife pond so enjoyable.

Animals – from hedgehogs (which are actually good swimmers), through to foxes, badgers and even fully grown deer – will visit your pond, provided they live in your vicinity and have access to the water.

All types of garden birds will seek out shallow areas where they can splash about in sunny weather – even during winter, for the cold does not deter them from taking a bath. Less welcome birds, such as herons, will also make regular calls, as long as there is a ready supply of food available to them.

Freshwater snails will probably need to be introduced to your pond either by accident or design (they can be purchased from aquatic centres, or they may come in unwittingly with water plants). They usually feed on decaying plant matter and algae. There are many different species of snail, some of which are tiny.

DO'S AND DON'TS FOR ATTRACTING WILDLIFE

- Do create an area of rockery near to the pond, which can offer sanctuary to amphibians, such as frogs, toads and newts.
- Don't have pools with steep sides, which makes it difficult for animals to get out of the water.
- Do create a central island within the pond; this can be a haven for small birds and insects.
- Don't stock large populations of ornamental fish, which will devour small creatures and plants.
- Do grow lush bog garden plants, with a good canopy of leaves, to give small creatures essential protection.
- Don't put the pond near to large trees, which would interrupt the flight access to waterfowl (more relevant to larger ponds).
- Do allow dead and decaying wood to become a feature of your wildlife pond; these places can support many types of insect, as well as fungi, mosses and lichens.
- Do – and perhaps this is the most important 'do' of all – create a sitting area, where you can observe (and feed) the wildlife at close quarters.

Troubleshooting

Maintaining a pond and various water garden plants will inevitably attract occasional pests, diseases and other problems. The following diagram is designed to help you diagnose some common pond-related problems from the symptoms you can observe. Starting with the plant or part of the pond that appears to be the most affected, by answering successive questions 'yes' [✓] or 'no' [✗] you will quickly arrive at a probable cause. Once you have identified the cause, turn to the relevant entry in the directory of pests and diseases for details of how to treat the problem.

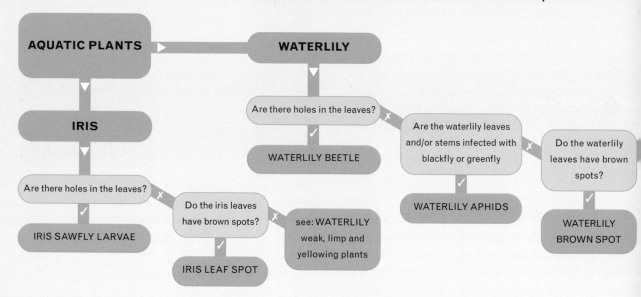

AQUATIC PLANTS → WATERLILY

WATERLILY → Are there holes in the leaves?
- ✓ WATERLILY BEETLE
- ✗ Are the waterlily leaves and/or stems infected with blackfly or greenfly
  - ✓ WATERLILY APHIDS
  - ✗ Do the waterlily leaves have brown spots?
    - ✓ WATERLILY BROWN SPOT

AQUATIC PLANTS → IRIS

IRIS → Are there holes in the leaves?
- ✓ IRIS SAWFLY LARVAE
- ✗ Do the iris leaves have brown spots?
  - ✓ IRIS LEAF SPOT
  - ✗ see: WATERLILY weak, limp and yellowing plants

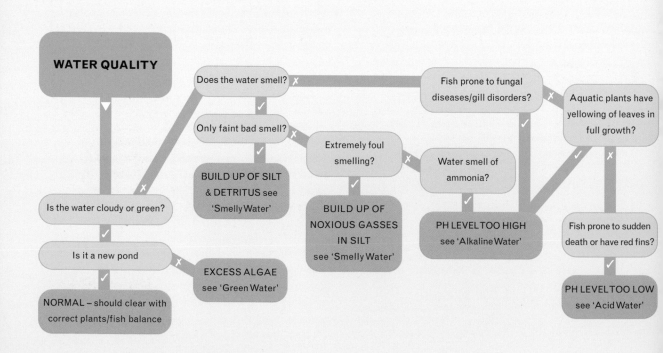

WATER QUALITY

Does the water smell?
- ✓ Only faint bad smell?
  - ✓ BUILD UP OF SILT & DETRITUS see 'Smelly Water'
  - ✗ Extremely foul smelling?
    - ✓ BUILD UP OF NOXIOUS GASSES IN SILT see 'Smelly Water'
    - ✗ Water smell of ammonia?
      - ✓ PH LEVEL TOO HIGH see 'Alkaline Water'
- ✗ Is the water cloudy or green?
  - ✓ Is it a new pond
    - ✓ NORMAL – should clear with correct plants/fish balance
    - ✗ EXCESS ALGAE see 'Green Water'

Fish prone to fungal diseases/gill disorders?
- ✓ ...
- ✗ Aquatic plants have yellowing of leaves in full growth?
  - ✓ ...
  - ✗ Fish prone to sudden death or have red fins?
    - ✓ PH LEVEL TOO LOW see 'Acid Water'

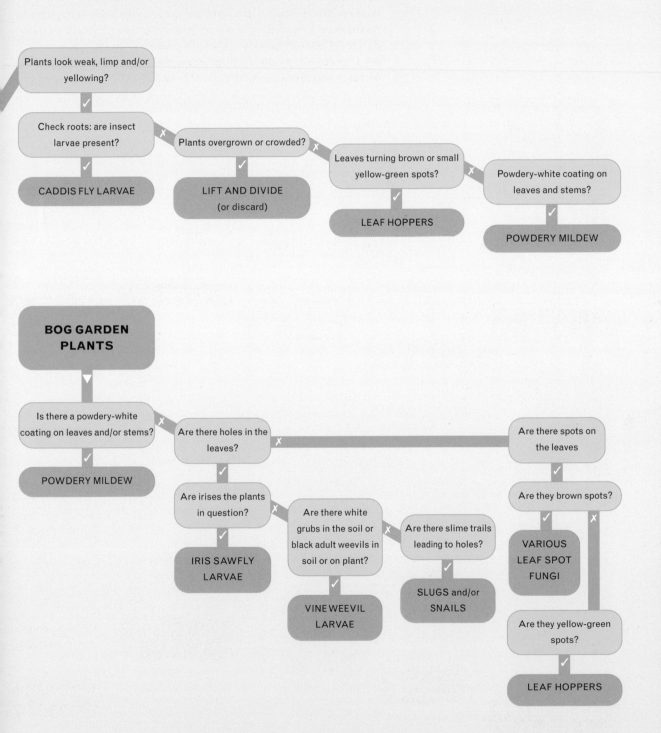

Plants look weak, limp and/or yellowing?

✓

Check roots: are insect larvae present?

✗

Plants overgrown or crowded?

✗

Leaves turning brown or small yellow-green spots?

✗

Powdery-white coating on leaves and stems?

✓

CADDIS FLY LARVAE

✓

LIFT AND DIVIDE
(or discard)

✓

LEAF HOPPERS

✓

POWDERY MILDEW

BOG GARDEN PLANTS

▽

Is there a powdery-white coating on leaves and/or stems?

✗

Are there holes in the leaves?

✗

Are there spots on the leaves

✓

POWDERY MILDEW

✓

Are irises the plants in question?

✗

Are they brown spots?

✓

Are there white grubs in the soil or black adult weevils in soil or on plant?

✗

Are there slime trails leading to holes?

✓

IRIS SAWFLY LARVAE

✓

VINE WEEVIL LARVAE

✓

SLUGS and/or SNAILS

✓ ✗

VARIOUS LEAF SPOT FUNGI

Are they yellow-green spots?

✓

LEAF HOPPERS

Water Garden Problems

All ponds and water features will at some time suffer problems. Either the water will become cloudy or green with algae, or it might smell, or the pond might leak, and so on. Rectifying all these problems is of course entirely possible, but might take time.

Acid water

When fish are prone to disease, sudden death and red fins, this is a sure sign that the water has a high level of acidity (or low pH). Other indications are when oxygenating plants do not multiply well, biological pond filters do not work properly, and water snails develop thin, pitted shells. Remedy: see 'Alkaline water' below.

Alkaline water

When fish are prone to fungal diseases and gill disorders, this is a sure sign that the water has a high level of alkalinity (or high pH). Other indications are when oxygenating plants are covered in a slimy coating, water plants display a yellowing of the leaves when in full growth, and the water smells slightly of ammonia. Remedy: Whether the water is biased towards acidity or alkalinity, the remedial process is the same. To correct the pH level so that it is as near to the desired level of pH7–7.5, start by changing about 25% of the water in the pond. Then increase the aeration level, such as by running a fountain or waterfall, turning on a filter or venturi aeration device.

Green water

Caused by a vast number of microscopic algae, this is not harmful to fish or plants, but is unsightly and detracts from the beauty of the garden. In new ponds this effect should clear by itself. If not, install a filter with UV clarifier, and then when the water has cleared by half or more, add more oxygenating plants to get nearer to the desirable 'balance' of plants to fish.

Smelly water

A balanced pond with fish, plants, and perhaps a fountain or cascade will have enough 'going on' to prevent the build up of gases. If your pond has just a faint odour, then reduce the water level by about half, and use a pond vacuum to suck up the silt and detritus from the bottom of the pond. Then, top up with clean water. If the problem is acute, it is probably caused by a lack of oxygen in the sediment, promoting the growth of certain bacteria, which produce unpleasant gases, such as methane and hydrogen sulphide – which smells of bad eggs. Drain the pond (after first netting out any fish), extract the silt, and refill it with clean water. Installing a filter with UV clarifier should help to prevent this from happening again.

Leaking concrete pond

To trace the leak, turn off all pumps and filters, and allow the water to drop to the level from where it is escaping. The leak may be in the rendering – caused by excessive exposure to sunlight or general wear and tear. Alternatively it may be in the base concrete, due to outside influences such as plant roots growing through it. A small leak can be repaired with an application of rendering. Where the leak is more serious it may be necessary to install a butyl liner as a membrane, which will maintain the water in the pond. Remember, if roots have caused the problem these will need treating before the liner is put in place. If not, they will continue to grow, and will damage the liner, causing the leak to start all over again.

Pond icing over

The ice layer prevents oxygen from getting in to the water as well as harmful gases being allowed to escape. If snow then falls, it will settle on the ice and prevent light from penetrating into the water for the fish. Melt a hole with a saucepan full of boiling water. Or prevent ice from forming in the first place by using an electric pool heater. Alternatively, run a fountain or waterfall permanently – the moving water never becomes still enough for ice to form.

Pests & Diseases of Aquatic Plants

Like all other garden plants, aquatics and bog garden types are subject to the ravages of specific pests and diseases. Fortunately, however, there are relatively few types that cause serious problems, and the control measures are some of the easiest for the gardener.

Blackfly/Greenfly

In a water garden situation these should be referred to more correctly as waterlily aphids. If plants are infested, spray the leaves forcefully with a jet of water to wash the flies into the pond where, with luck, any fish will eat them. However, because these aphids are flying insects, it is likely that your plants will receive further infestations during the growing season.

Waterlilly beetle

The small brown beetles are the most damaging pest of waterlilies. The adult beetle lays its eggs on the leaves in early summer, and then the blackish larvae emerge. These grubs eat the leaves, making holes on the edges as well as in the centres. Eventually the leaf becomes so damaged that it withers and rots in the water. Cut away badly affected leaves, and hose the grubs into the water.

Caddis fly

The larva, or 'stick grub', of this insect chews into the roots of aquatic plants to make a shelter. Some plants may suffer a little damage, but it only becomes serious if a large number of the grubs are present. There is no recommended treatment for the control of the flies. In any case, if there are fish present, the grubs soon become a useful source of food.

Iris sawfly

The larva of this insect is a bluish maggot, which feeds on the leaves of irises. During the summer it will eat holes in the edges of the leaves; a second generation may do the same during autumn. Remove seriously damaged leaves, and pick off and destroy any grubs seen. Where bog garden irises are affected, an application of derris dust will help to control the pest.

Leaf hoppers

These small, green, hopping insects move from plant to plant, and they do most damage to soft, fleshy-leaved marginals at the edges of our ponds. Affected leaves will have small pale yellow-green spots on the upper leaf surfaces; in bad cases the whole leaf will turn brown. Hose the grubs into the water, where they will be consumed by fish or frogs.

Slugs/garden snails

These do not cause a problem in the water, but they can devour precious plants at the water's edge or in the bog garden. Chemical control is by means of brightly coloured pellets, but these are thought to be harmful to birds and other creatures that might be tempted to eat the deceased molluscs. Laying beer or orange peel traps overnight, for collecting and destroying the assembled molluscs in the morning, is a more environmentally friendly, if unpleasant form of control. In fact, bog gardens – which of course are moist, dank and often shaded – are perfect breeding grounds for these pests.

Vine weevils

Bog garden plants are at risk here; the adult weevils gnaw holes in leaves of hostas, aruncus, astilbes and sometimes primulas. The cream coloured grubs are more damaging in that they eat the roots of certain plants, often causing the death of the plant. They are a particular problem in containerized garden plants. Remove and destroy the adult weevils by hand. In cases of severe infestation, drench the soil with a systemic insecticide containing imidacloprid, but do not use this if there is any chance whatsoever of run-off into the pond.

Index of Plants

This index lists the plants mentioned in this book by their Latin names. Common names appear in bold type where applicable

General Index

Acknowledgements

The author and publishers would like to thank Coolings Nurseries for their cooperation and assistance with the photography in this book, including the loan of tools and much specialist equipment. Special thanks go to Sandra Gratwick and Mark Reeve. Coolings Nurseries Ltd., Rushmore Hill, Knockholt, Kent, TN14 7NN. Tel: 00 44 1959 532269; Email: coolings@coolings.co.uk; Website: www.coolings.co.uk. Thanks are also due to Paul Dalton, Kevin Dodson and Greg Wallbridge of Maidenhead Aquatics, Polhill Garden Centre, Badgers Mount, Sevenoaks, Kent TN14 7BD for their assistance with the practical photography in this book.

The publishers would also like to thank the following companies and individuals for supplying images for this book: Stapeley Water Gardens of Nantwich, Cheshire, for a number of the plant portraits that appear throughout the A–Z sections of this book; Hozelock Ltd for the images on pages 12 (top); 17; 28 (bottom left); and 31: Geoff Sample, for the photograph of the frog on page 152; and finally, Mark Baker for the photograph of the pond skater on page 153.